BE
ASTONISHING

SOUND WISDOM BOOK BY SAM SILVERSTEIN AND DR. ALLISON SILVERSTEIN

Be Astonishing: How to Transform Ordinary Influence Into Lasting Significance

SOUND WISDOM BOOKS BY SAM SILVERSTEIN

The Theory of Accountability: Building a Truly Accountable, High-Performance, High-Growth Life for Yourself and Your Organization

The Accountability Advantage: Design a Sustainable, High-Performance Culture to Build Stronger Businesses, Communities, and People

The Accountability Circle: Discovering Your True Purpose, Potential, and Impact—with Accountability Partnerships

PIVOT! Three Big Questions that Reframe Your Perspective, Maximize Your Potential, and Improve Your Life

Momentum: How to Avoid Going in the Wrong Direction

*I Am Accountable: Ten Choices That Create Deeper Meaning
in Your Life, Your Organization, and Your World*

The Lost Commandments

*No More Excuses! The Five Accountabilities for
Personal and Organizational Growth*

No Matter What: The 10 Commitments of Accountability

The Success Model: Five Steps to Revolutionize Your Life

Making Accountable Decisions: A Journey to an Accountable Life

*Non-Negotiable: The Story of Happy State
Bank & the Power of Accountability*

BE
ASTONISHING

HOW TO TRANSFORM ORDINARY INFLUENCE INTO LASTING SIGNIFICANCE

SAM SILVERSTEIN
DR. ALLISON SILVERSTEIN

Published and distributed by:

SOUND WISDOM
P.O. Box 310
Shippensburg, PA 17257-0310
717-530-2122

info@soundwisdom.com

www.soundwisdom.com

While efforts have been made to verify information contained in this publication, neither the author nor the publisher assumes any responsibility for errors, inaccuracies, or omissions. While this publication is chock-full of useful, practical information; it is not intended to be legal or accounting advice. All readers are advised to seek competent lawyers and accountants to follow laws and regulations that may apply to specific situations. The reader of this publication assumes responsibility for the use of the information. The author and publisher assume no responsibility or liability whatsoever on the behalf of the reader of this publication.

ISBN 13 TP: 978-1-6409-5583-7

ISBN 13 eBook: 978-1-6409-5584-4

For Worldwide Distribution, Printed in the U.S.A.

1 2 3 4 5 6 7 8 / 29 28 27 26 25

DEDICATION

For our beloved parents and grandparents — Your lives have shown us that hard work with integrity, determination with purpose, and love shared along the way create the richest kind of success. Working side by side with trust and dedication, you turned challenges into achievements and modeled the joy of building something together. You gave us roots in perseverance and wings to pursue our own paths.

With gratitude and love,
Sam & Allison

CONTENTS

Chapter 1

IN THE BEGINNING: THE POWER OF THUNDER

THE QUIET FORCE OF BEING ASTONISHING

To meet Dr. Laurie Sherlock is to encounter a quiet force, one whose impact is felt not in grand pronouncements, but in the steady, intentional way she shows up for people, over and over again. She doesn't need to say she's astonishing; in fact, she would openly deny it if asked. However, it's written in the lives she touches, the teams she transforms, and the unwavering way she believes in the good.

I (AS) first met Laurie in her role as a neonatologist, a physician dedicated to the care of some of the most medically fragile newborns. She personifies the quote "Some people create so much light that all around them grow," by a small inspirational card company, Curly Girl Design. To say Laurie is respected by her colleagues would be an understatement; the admiration they hold for her borders on reverence, reserved only for the rarest of individuals.

Laurie approaches clinical care with a quiet intensity, a steady grace, and an intentionality that shows what medicine can be at its most human. Laurie stands beside families during their most difficult days, offering not just expertise but presence. What makes Laurie astonishing is not just what she does, but who she is in the doing. She brings her whole self into rooms, her clarity, her conviction, her compassion, and leaves people changed. She offers emotional courage without fanfare, strategic wisdom without ego, and love without condition.

Laurie isn't just someone you're glad to work alongside; she's someone who makes you want to be more generous, more grounded, more real. Her character and impact became immediately apparent during our interview together.

A commitment to lifting others became a throughline in Laurie's life, showing up in how she mothers, mentors, and leads. She speaks about each of her children with joy, insight, and an almost sacred attentiveness. She celebrates their independence, their empathy, their defiance, their steadiness, many qualities that echo her own.

Laurie's leadership is grounded not in hierarchy but in humanity. She describes her unique purpose this way: "To help people see the good in them, and hope that in seeing the good in them, they're able to spread good in their own spheres." That's the ripple effect Laurie believes in, the idea that love, when rooted in authenticity, can multiply.

And yet, even with all her wisdom, Laurie remains refreshingly humble. "I don't know what made me that way," she admitted when asked how she came to light up through uplifting others. But then she quietly traced the lineage back to her parents, who prioritized kindness and lifting up one another. Her story is one of becoming,

Love, when rooted in authenticity, can multiply.

of learning to see that "the horizontal outreach and love we can give to each other can have more of a ripple effect." Laurie asserts, "By turning my heart to search for the good, I almost always find it, which means I am constantly finding and encountering light, lifting me up. It helps me too (so not pure altruism by any stretch) to seek to see the good and beauty in everyone else."

Central to her story, and yet not at all a prerequisite to her being the astonishing human she is today, was an accident. Laurie was a pedestrian hit by a car when she was almost 35 weeks pregnant with a baby boy. From this event, she and her husband lost their son, Edison, and Laurie faced an immense physical recovery with over 30 broken bones. This was a moment that could have defined her by limitation, yet instead became a testament to her remarkable resilience and grace.

After the accident, Laurie faced not only physical recovery but an emotional and spiritual journey. The experience challenged her in ways that most people never encounter, shaking the very foundation of her life and work. Rather than allowing trauma to harden her, Laurie allowed it to deepen her empathy and expand her understanding of human fragility and strength. She came to embody what she had always believed, that vulnerability is not weakness, it's a doorway to connection and healing.

A core part of her approach is creating a sense of safety that allows someone to feel vulnerable enough to tell the truth about what's really going on. And who better to understand that need than someone who has lived through her own vulnerability so profoundly?

Laurie's astonishing nature shines brightest in how she integrates this personal hardship into her professional mission and her daily life. It fuels her authenticity, her insistence that the love and care she offers must be genuine, because "If it's not genuine, people don't believe you." It informs her belief in the power of lifting up others.

The accident is not a detour from Laurie's path, nor is it the cover of her book, but merely a chapter, an event that refined her extraordinary capacity to serve, to lead, and to inspire. Her story reminds us that astonishing people respond with courage, compassion, and an unwavering commitment to the good in themselves and others when facing challenges. Laurie had an acceleration of knowledge as a result of the accident. She learned about suffering and how to sit in darkness with others, skills she would hone both personally and professionally.

After the accident, in her path to parenthood, Laurie connected with fierce, generous women who chose to become surrogates,

Vulnerability is not weakness, it's a doorway to connection and healing.

Astonishing people respond with courage, compassion, and an unwavering commitment to the good in themselves and others when facing challenges.

---

offering their bodies, their strength, and their hearts so another family could be born. It was an experience that shattered assumptions and redefined love, trust, and the boundaries of connection. Laurie marveled, "It's a huge, huge medical commitment to grow a child that you are not biologically related to…that to me is an astonishing human being."

Laurie and her children regularly talk to their surrogate mothers and have even traveled together. Laurie's story is a special tribute to the quiet heroism of others, and to the courage it takes to believe, even through heartbreak, that the astonishing is still possible.

Laurie is a powerful example of what it means to move through life not just surviving, but transforming every space you enter. There comes a moment, rare, electric, when someone doesn't just enter the room, they *change* it. Something shifts. Eyes lift. The air feels different.

This is what it means to be astonishing: to consistently embody principles that inspire, uplift, and empower others, creating positive change and a lasting impact. Not loud for the sake of volume, but thunderous in impact, so surprisingly powerful, so deeply true, that it overwhelms and awakens.

From the Latin *tonare*, "to thunder," being astonishing is not about applause or spotlight. It is about becoming a force, undeniable, unforgettable, that stirs others to rise, think, and transform. This book is your invitation to bring that thunder to the world.

So, how do you discover your gift and release your thunder? Sometimes, someone else sees it before you do. A teacher, a friend, a mentor, someone who recognizes a spark in you and calls it out. Other times, you are the one who sees it in someone else and gives

There comes a moment, rare, electric, when someone doesn't just enter the room, they change it.

This is what it means to be astonishing: to consistently embody principles that inspire, uplift, and empower others, creating positive change and a lasting impact.

them the courage to believe. Either way, discovering your gift is not a one-time event. It's not a destination. It's a way of being, a lifelong unfolding of potential and purpose.

What separates an astonishing person from the rest? It's not money or status or a long list of accolades. Astonishing people walk through the world with certain unmistakable traits: they are passionate, authentic, curious, resilient, hard workers who are committed to the well-being of others. Their presence changes the temperature of a room. When you're around them, you feel seen. You feel like anything is possible. You feel better about who *you* are.

Astonishing people contribute to and are part of building an accountable world. They stand out, not because they try to be different, but because they operate at a profoundly higher level. They make a tangible impact on the lives of those around them. They are the people you believe in, because they believe in you, too. And they are constantly asking themselves: *How can I be better? How can I love more? How can I rise after falling? How can I contribute more deeply and live more fully?*

The question becomes: *are you simply raising the floor*, making sure no one falls, *or are you raising the ceiling*, expanding what's possible, even if it means risking failure along the way?

Being astonishing isn't about playing it safe. It's about daring to lift yourself and others beyond limits, creating space for growth, courage, and unexpected breakthroughs. It is choosing the path that challenges and stretches you, because that is where true impact lives.

Being astonishing is not about applause or spotlight. It is about becoming a force, undeniable, unforgettable, that stirs others to rise, think, and transform.

The question becomes: are you simply raising the floor, making sure no one falls, or are you raising the ceiling, expanding what's possible, even if it means risking failure along the way?

Join us as we uncover the qualities that define truly astonishing individuals and organizations, and discover how you can bring these traits into your everyday life and share your thunder with the world.

Chapter 2

LAYING THE GROUNDWORK: INTRODUCTION TO THE ASTONISHING PRINCIPLES

Be Astonishing is more than a guide, it is a blueprint for transforming your life and organization in extraordinary ways. The book is structured into six principles that lay the groundwork for this astonishing transformation. Each principle builds upon the last, forming a deliberate sequence that takes you step by step toward unleashing your greatest impact.

The seeds for the principles already exist within each one of us. We just need to recognize them, nurture them, and learn how to develop them. That's what this book is all about, helping you see the potential you already possess and guiding you through the process of cultivating it. This is your opportunity to become a catalyst for growth, connection, and inspiration. This is your opportunity to tap into something bigger than yourself, unleashing your own thunder.

Through powerful real-life stories, you'll see these principles in action, how individuals and organizations have embraced them to achieve remarkable results. These stories have been deliberately chosen to provide practical insights you can apply immediately, helping you bring these principles to life in your own journey.

The journey begins with "Fuel Your Fire," igniting the deep passion within yourself that drives you toward what truly matters to you. This passion not only impacts your personal experiences but also spreads to those around you, lifting up others and empowering them.

Next comes the importance of "Free Your Mindset." To be truly astonishing, you must free yourself from the limitations that hold you back. Often, the biggest limitation is your own belief in what is possible. Freeing your mindset allows you to shift your reality and see what is in front of you.

To compound the power of passion and perspective, you must "Outwork Your Ordinary," turning consistent effort into astonishing growth. It is not about being the hardest-working person on the planet or burning yourself out every single day, it is about putting in the effort to outwork *your* ordinary. It's about showing up every day and doing a little bit more.

Of course, no journey of growth is frictionless. Along the way, you will face numerous challenges. That is why it is of paramount importance for you to "Forge Your Resilience." Resilience is not only bouncing back but also using setbacks as fuel for even greater success. It is your foundation, allowing you to rise stronger after each challenge, empowering you to continue making progress even in the face of difficulty.

Through the process, it is imperative that you remain your truest self and "Live Your Authenticity." When you show up as your authentic

No journey of growth is frictionless.

self, you create genuine connections with others, building trust and inspiring loyalty. Authenticity brings a sense of clarity and purpose to everything you do—and most importantly, it's contagious. When your actions align with your true self, you inspire others to embrace the same.

Finally, we discuss the value of knowing how to "Love People," which is all about genuinely caring for those around you. This involves taking the time to understand a person's needs, supporting their growth, and helping them realize their potential. When you love and care for others in this way, you not only elevate their lives but also create a ripple effect of positivity and empowerment that can transform teams, organizations, and communities.

Be Astonishing is designed to help you unlock your fullest potential and achieve lasting transformation. You will learn how to apply the principles to your life and organization, creating an environment where greatness is nurtured and extraordinary results become the standard. We offer you the tools to not only achieve success but also to redefine what success looks like for you. By truly living these tenets, you will discover what it means to become astonishing.

Our advice is to use the book in two distinct ways.

First, read the book as an overarching story, understanding the principles and how they build upon each other. Let it inspire you, helping you see the possibilities for profound change in both your personal life and within your organization. As you read, allow the stories and insights to shift your mindset and spark your imagination for the transformation ahead.

Second, revisit the principles as you begin implementing them in your life. Each time you encounter a challenge or seek growth, return to the principles, reflecting on how they apply in new contexts. This process will help you continuously evolve, ensuring that each experience you face becomes an opportunity for deeper understanding and progress.

As you begin to embody these principles in every aspect of your life, you will continually become more astonishing. Your personal journey of transformation is just the beginning; with each principle you apply, you will discover new ways to inspire and uplift those around you.

For now, relax and enjoy learning about the power of thunder.

Chapter 3

FUEL YOUR FIRE

Fueling your fire is aligning your actions with a passion you discover within you. Passion is a deep, internal drive fueled by personal meaning and emotional connection. It is a consistent enthusiasm or strong inclination toward a subject, activity, or cause. Passion isn't just liking something, it's feeling compelled to engage, contribute, and persevere even through difficulty.

In all the people and organizations we researched and spoke with, there was a commonality present. People discovered a need—whether it be the desire for a locally owned and operated bank, more accessible eyewear, or the availability of quality healthcare. It became about serving others. People were at the center of everything.

Your fire is fueled when you have alignment between your values, purpose, and actions. It often feels like a "calling," something you must do, not just something you choose to do.

Passion is the emotional fuel that transforms effort into fulfillment and persistence into mastery.

Fueling your fire is aligning your actions with a passion you discover within you.

It is also directional; it energizes and focuses attention on what matters most. It's rooted in curiosity, personal experiences, and sometimes pain or injustice you feel driven to resolve.

Passionate individuals often become role models and catalysts for others. Passionate leaders build cultures of purpose and energy that inspire high performance and accountability. It creates magnetic energy that employees, clients, and stakeholders want to be around. Leaders who infuse passion into their organization create an environment that always attracts and retains the best people. Customers and clients will flock to do business with you.

An organization aligned with collective passion operates with greater clarity and cohesion. It fosters loyalty, engagement, and a willingness to go the extra mile. Passion drives innovation by encouraging curiosity and the courage to challenge the status quo. Teams that are passionate about their mission are more resilient in the face of adversity.

This is the first piece of the puzzle toward being astonishing because it ignites everything else. Without passion, effort becomes obligation, ideas lose their edge, and work begins to feel hollow.

But when passion is present, it breathes life into action. It gives you stamina when the road is long, clarity when the path is murky, and conviction when others doubt.

Passion doesn't just fuel productivity, it fuels purpose. Passion is the spark that sets the astonishing in motion; it's where the extraordinary begins.

DESIGNING YOUR PASSION

Melanie Perkins was frustrated that graphic design software was so complex that it felt out of reach for most people. The average person couldn't easily create something visually appealing, whether for a party invitation or a social media post, because the tools were too difficult to use.

With this challenge in mind, Melanie, along with her husband Cliff Obrecht and Cameron Adams, launched Canva in 2013. Canva

---

Passion is the emotional fuel that transforms effort into fulfillment and persistence into mastery.

Passion is the spark that sets the astonishing in motion; it's where the extraordinary begins.

is an online design and visual communication platform with a mission to empower everyone in the world to design anything and publish anywhere. Today, this software is used by more than 220 million people in more than 190 countries. From students to professionals, the Canva platform has become the de facto design standard globally.

Canva has what they call a "Two-Step Plan." They are driven by a deeper purpose: Step One is to build one of the world's most valuable companies; Step Two is to use that success to do the most good they can. Step One is about empowering the world to design. Step Two is about giving back. They believe that the more they grow, the more good they can do.

Passion was at the heart of Canva's birth, which remains central to how they operate today. For example, they were the first Australian company to sign The Climate Pledge and have planted well over 10 million trees. Their stated value, to be a force for good, brings Canva's people together, creating a special place to work. Passion flows through their culture, the services they offer, and the way in which they connect to the world. It's this passion that *fuels the fire* in their people, the fire to create an astonishing organization and the fire to have an astonishing impact on their community, the world.

Passion fuels perseverance, making it easier to push through obstacles and setbacks. It elevates the quality of work; people who care deeply are more likely to innovate and go above and beyond. Passion creates authenticity; people are drawn to those who are genuinely committed and enthusiastic. It unlocks intrinsic motivation, reducing dependency on external validation or rewards. And, passion leads to a sense of meaning and significance in work and life.

PASSION, MD

After getting married at age 9, at just 14 years old, Dr. Anandi Gopal Joshi gave birth to a son. Due to a lack of access to proper medical care, she watched helplessly as her baby died only 10 days later. Such a profound loss at a young age could have broken anyone's spirit, especially in a time and place where women were offered few rights or opportunities. But instead of being defeated by her circumstances, Dr. Joshi transformed her grief into a passionate drive to change not only her own future but also the lives of countless others.

When most girls were still in school and discovering who they were socially, Dr. Joshi began the process of educating herself. Her experience with the death of her child exposed her to the dire need for proper medical care, and it was then that she resolved to become a doctor. This decision was nothing short of radical in a society where women, especially young girls, were expected to accept their roles within the confines of domesticity and not seek roles in fields traditionally dominated by men.

Instead of allowing the constraints of society control her life, Dr. Joshi took every challenge and converted it into fuel for her passion. She pushed forward, pursuing her dream to study medicine. Through sheer resilience, she earned a scholarship to study at the Women's Medical College of Pennsylvania, a feat that seemed impossible at the time for a girl from India. Ultimately, she became the first Indian female doctor of Western medicine.

Dr. Joshi's story is a testament to fueling your fire. Her fire was not simply born from the ambition to achieve personal success, but from enduring pain she did not want anyone else to go through.

Though she died tragically young at the age of 21, Dr. Joshi left behind a legacy that continues to inspire. Her courage laid the foundation for generations of Indian women to dream bigger, to fight harder, and to believe that no matter how impossible the path may seem, change is always within reach when driven by passion and purpose.

TAPPING INTO YOUR FIRE

When you can understand and tap into the passion within you, you will not only transform yourself but also those around you. To discover the depth of your passion, think about the following:

Individually:

- Reflect on moments when you felt most energized or fulfilled; what were you doing, and why did it matter?

- Identify activities that feel effortless and make time disappear; these are passion indicators.

- Explore pain points or injustices that stir you emotionally; they may hold clues to a deeper purpose.

- Ask, "What would I still do if I never got paid?" or "What do I talk about even when I'm not asked?"

- Take note of what angers or frustrates you in the world; your passion may lie in being part of the solution.

- Examine what makes you proud; past achievements often point toward passion.

- Give yourself permission to experiment and follow curiosity without the pressure of immediate clarity.

As a leader:

- Reconnect with the original "why" behind your organization's founding or your leadership journey.

- Identify what aspects of leadership bring you the most joy or pride; mentoring, building teams, solving complex problems, etc.

- Spend time listening to stories from team members; see what resonates and reawakens your sense of purpose.

- Align your daily responsibilities with your values and vision whenever possible.

- Seek feedback about the impact you've had; it often reveals where your passion is felt most.

- Reframe challenges as opportunities to act on your passion, not just fix problems.

- Periodically unplug from routine to reflect and reignite your internal spark.

WAVES OF PASSION

The moment we discover what truly ignites our passion is unlike any other. It's as if a light suddenly turns on, casting clarity over our lives and aligning our purpose with something greater than ourselves. This kind of realization doesn't just motivate us, it defines us.

For Bethany Hamilton, that light came early. Born in 1990 in Hawaii and raised in a family of surfers, Bethany was drawn to the ocean from the start. Surfing wasn't just a hobby for her, it was a calling. From the feel of the board beneath her feet to the rhythm of the waves, everything about surfing made her feel alive. It empowered her. It was where she felt most herself. By the age of 13, her passion had already placed her in national competitions and on a trajectory toward professional success.

Then, in an instant, everything changed. A 14-foot shark attack resulted in the loss of her left arm, an injury that, for many, would mark the end of their dreams. But for Bethany, the love for surfing was too strong to let go. The question wasn't whether she could come back. It was how soon she could return to what she was most passionate about.

Just 26 days after the attack, Bethany was back on her board, not because she needed to prove something to the world, but because she couldn't imagine life without surfing. Her passion was the compass that guided her recovery, the anchor that kept her grounded, and the spark that gave her hope. Surfing wasn't just something she did, it was part of who she was.

In 2005, she claimed her first major win at the NSSA National Championship. But even more than her titles, what stood out was her unwavering connection to the ocean and to her sport. Bethany didn't return to surfing to chase medals. She returned because her passion never left her.

Over time, that passion expanded into a mission. Through the Bethany Hamilton Foundation, she now shares the joy and empowerment of surfing with others, especially youth and individuals with disabilities, so they too can discover the transformative power of finding what they love.

Bethany Hamilton's story is not just one of perseverance, it's a celebration of passion. Her journey shows us that when you truly love something, that love can carry you through the darkest of times.

Passion isn't just about the spark that starts the fire; it's about the energy that keeps it burning.

Passion isn't just about the spark that starts the fire; it's about the energy that keeps it burning.

Bethany Hamilton teaches us that passion isn't just a private force, it's a contagious one. Astonishing people don't just discover and pursue their passion, they live it out loud. They share it, lead with it, and inspire others to uncover their own. Bethany's love for surfing became a platform to empower youth and redefine what's possible, not only for herself but for countless others. This is the power of passion when it's lived with purpose.

PASSION IN PRACTICE: PARTNERS IN HEALTH

Founded by Dr. Paul Farmer, Ophelia Dahl, and Jim Yong Kim, Partners In Health (PIH) is a global health organization relentlessly

Astonishing people don't just discover and pursue their passion, they live it out loud.

committed to bringing high-quality healthcare to the poorest and most marginalized communities around the world.

PIH's approach is grounded in the belief that every person, regardless of income, geography, or social status, deserves not just access to care, but access to the *best* care. Their work is fueled by moral imagination and a fierce sense of justice, not just technical expertise.

PIH's passion isn't just emotional, it's fiercely intellectual and deeply ethical. The organization challenges global norms, pushes for systemic reform, and refuses to accept the status quo of health disparities. They pair medical excellence with social justice, understanding that treating a disease without addressing the conditions that caused it is never enough.

PIH's staff, from doctors and community health workers to logisticians and engineers, live this passion daily. Many work in crisis zones and underserved areas not for prestige or high pay, but because they believe health is a human right, and that dignity must be woven into every part of care. They treat patients with compassion and respect, and they stay for the long haul, through hurricanes, cholera outbreaks, and political instability, because they are invested not just in outcomes, but in people.

Perhaps most astonishing is how PIH channels this passion into partnership. They don't swoop in with temporary fixes; they work alongside local governments, train national staff, and help strengthen health systems from the ground up. Passion is sustainable when it is shared, cultivated within communities who rise as co-leaders in the work.

In the face of despair, PIH's passion is stubborn. It's hopeful. It's relentless. And it reminds the world that caring deeply, unreasonably, unapologetically, and persistently, can save lives, change systems, and reimagine what is possible.

AS A LEADER, HOW DO YOU HELP OTHERS FUEL THEIR FIRE?

As leaders, we have a unique opportunity, and responsibility, to help others fuel their fire. It starts with creating an environment where curiosity, exploration, and self-expression are welcomed. People need to feel safe before they can be bold. Ask meaningful questions such as, "What gives you energy?" or "What do you care about most here?" These aren't just icebreakers, they're invitations to connect with purpose.

Give your team room to grow through stretch assignments, cross-functional projects, or passion initiatives that allow them to tap

Passion is sustainable when it is shared, cultivated within communities who rise as co-leaders in the work.

into their strengths. Help them see how their unique contributions align with a larger mission. When people understand *why* their work matters, passion becomes part of the process, not just the outcome.

And most importantly, model it. Show your team what it looks like to be on fire for something. Share stories of impact, purpose, and transformation. Create opportunities for reflection and exploration, whether it's through mentorship, side projects, or volunteering. When people are supported in discovering what drives them, they don't just perform better, they lead with greater authenticity and inspire those around them.

Organizations that intentionally cultivate passion among their people are not only more innovative, they're more resilient, energized, and purpose-driven. Passionate organizations celebrate individuality while aligning personal drive with collective purpose. They understand that when people are encouraged to lead from their strengths and contribute in ways that matter to them, engagement deepens, collaboration strengthens, and the entire organization thrives. Passion, when supported at the organizational level, becomes a powerful force for transformation, from the inside out.

A culture that fuels passion is a culture that multiplies impact.

HOW TO FUEL YOUR FIRE

Passion isn't found, it's cultivated. The astonishing people and organizations in this chapter didn't wait to feel inspired. They acted. They created. They endured. And in doing so, they uncovered a fire that guided everything else.

The following are seven steps to take toward fueling your fire and living an astonishing life:

1. Pay Attention to What Moves You

Notice the moments that energize you, frustrate you, or stir something deep. Passion often hides in your emotions.

Dr. Anandi Gopal Joshi didn't just suffer loss, she channeled it. Her grief became a mission to protect and heal others.

2. Use Pain as a Spark, Not a Stop Sign

Hardship can ignite passion if you let it. Don't waste your wounds, turn them into fuel.

Bethany Hamilton could've quit after the shark attack. Instead, she made her comeback part of her story and used it to lift up others.

3. Revisit What You Loved Before You Were Told Who to Be

Think back to what lit you up before the world told you to be practical. Passion often lives where curiosity once thrived.

Melanie Perkins saw complexity in design software and remembered that creativity should feel fun and accessible.

4. Follow the Problems That Bother You Most

What injustice or inefficiency drives you crazy? That frustration might be your fire waiting to be focused.

PIH didn't just witness injustice, they were compelled to respond. Their mission was rooted in an unshakable refusal to look away.

5. Experiment Without the Pressure to Get It Right

You don't need clarity to begin. Start where you are, follow your curiosity, and let the clarity come later.

Canva started with one bold idea: design should be simple and available to everyone. That experiment became a revolution.

6. Turn Passion Into Practice

Fire fades without fuel. Keep it burning by putting it to work, in your role, your relationships, and your daily routines.

PIH didn't just care about health justice, they built systems, trained partners, and made it real.

7. Help Others Find Their Fire Too

Passion multiplies when it's shared. Create environments where people can connect to their own "why."

Bethany Hamilton didn't stop at surfing. She started a foundation to help others heal through the same waves that saved her.

BRINGING IT TOGETHER

To be astonishing, you must fuel your fire and protect it.

Passion isn't a luxury or a personality trait. It's a decision. A practice. A commitment to care deeply, act boldly, and persist faithfully. It's the energy that gets you up when you fall, the reason behind the late nights, and the power that transforms good work into meaningful impact.

Astonishing people, from Dr. Joshi and Bethany Hamilton to Canva's founders and the teams at PIH, aren't just fueled by what they love. They're driven by what they believe. They've aligned their fire with purpose. And that's what sustains them.

So ask yourself:

- What makes me come alive?

- What breaks my heart that I can help fix?

- What would I still do, even if no one paid me or noticed?

Because when your fire is rooted in meaning, not ego...

When your work is aligned with your values...

When your impact is born from conviction...

You don't just chase astonishing—you ignite it.

Chapter 4

FREE YOUR MINDSET

To be astonishing is to think beyond boundaries, question what's accepted, and envision what others are too afraid, or too conditioned, to imagine. "Free your mindset" is not a slogan—it's a call to revolutionize how you see limitations, not as end points but as the beginning of invention.

The world tells us, "This is how it's always been." Astonishing people ask, "But does it have to be?"

To *free your mindset* means to break free from the mental barriers, limitations, and beliefs that hold you back from seeing possibilities and achieving your true potential. It's about challenging the status quo and questioning the assumptions you've accepted as truths.

Freeing your mindset involves letting go of fixed thinking and embracing a more open, flexible, and growth-oriented perspective. It's about being willing to see the world differently, think creatively, and explore new ways of solving problems—even when it means going against conventional wisdom or facing adversity. It's a mindset shift from "I can't" to "What if?" that empowers you to innovate, take risks, and push beyond the boundaries of what's comfortable or expected.

Freeing your mindset isn't about being rebellious for the sake of it. It's about daring to think beyond the limits you've inherited, so you can build something better. Whether you're trying to change your life, your community, or the world.

INVENTING AGAINST THE ODDS

Sand. Rags. Grass. Newspaper. In the 1990s, in rural India, these were common substitutes for sanitary napkins. Commercial pads were unaffordable, and menstruation was taboo, silencing discussion and trapping women in unsafe, unhygienic practices. The result:

To be astonishing is to think beyond boundaries, question what's accepted, and envision what others are too afraid, or too conditioned, to imagine.

poor health and risk for infection, shame, and widespread neglect, accepted as normal.

But Arunachalam Muruganantham refused to accept that reality. When he discovered his wife using dirty rags, he decided to act. With no formal education or experience, he began experimenting with pad prototypes. After multiple failures, family members refused to keep helping; volunteers were too embarrassed by the stigma. He eventually created a device to test pads on himself, only to be mocked and ostracized by his village.

Still, he persisted. Once you see possibilities previously unseen, it is impossible to go back to how things were.

After years of trial and error, Muruganantham built a low-cost machine, just $750 compared to $400,000 for imported ones, that could produce sanitary pads. He founded Jayaashree Industries and began selling the machines to women's self-help groups across India. He turned down commercial offers, staying committed to his mission: affordable pads for all, made by the communities who need them.

His machines now reach millions, improving menstrual health and creating jobs for rural women. Celebrated as "Padman," Muruganantham's work has been chronicled in films, documentaries, and honored with the Padma Shri award. He freed his mindset, and in doing so, helped millions of others do the same.

Muruganantham didn't set out to change the world, he just wanted to help his wife and sisters. But in asking the kind of questions most people were too embarrassed to even consider, he exposed a silent crisis in women's health and dignity. The world laughed at him, rejected him, and called him crazy. And still, he kept going. Why? Because he had freed his mind from the trap of shame and conformity. He believed that real intelligence isn't about status or schooling, it's about empathy, persistence, and the refusal to look away. In a culture that told him "this is not your problem," he made it his mission.

Most people live within inherited boundaries, cultural, economic, educational, or emotional. These boundaries shape what we think is possible, acceptable, or even worth trying. But astonishing people question those boundaries. They don't just ask, *What is?* They ask, *What could be?* And then they *go there*, not because it's safe, but because it's necessary.

This story shows us what's possible when we dare to let go of the familiar script. To free your mindset is to see potential where others see impossibility. It's not easy. But it's necessary, because astonishing people don't just adapt to the world. They change it.

BRICK BY BRICK

Toys are more than playthings, they spark imagination, creativity, and learning. For many of us, childhood is inseparable from the toys that shaped our early experiences. But for some children, access to toys, especially educational ones like LEGO bricks, is limited by cost.

Charlie Jeffers, a lifelong LEGO enthusiast, understood how powerful these tiny bricks could be. As he grew older, he noticed friends discarding old sets and realized that many children could benefit from them. Instead of letting them go to waste, Charlie saw an opportunity.

He founded Pass The Bricks, a community-driven initiative to collect, sanitize, and redistribute used LEGO sets to children in need. Starting with grassroots outreach, door-knocking, social media, and

To free your mindset is to see potential where others see impossibility.

local volunteering, Charlie built a team of 25 volunteers who helped clean, sort, and repackage the sets with instructions and themes to foster creative, educational play.

By 2025, Pass The Bricks had donated more than 25,000 LEGO sets, weighing more than 12,200 pounds, to children in 193 cities worldwide.

Charlie's story is a testament to the power of freeing your mindset, from scarcity to abundance, from ownership to sharing. Charlie recognized that something as simple as LEGOs, which had brought him so much joy and creativity, could be transformed into a tool for spreading happiness and learning.

Rather than seeing his collection of LEGOs as just toys, he saw them as an opportunity to enrich the lives of others. What began as a simple idea became a global effort rooted in love, creativity, and generosity. He didn't just give away toys, he gave others the tools to dream. By freeing his mindset from a narrow focus on his own possessions, Charlie created a ripple effect of kindness and generosity.

TAPPING INTO YOUR MINDSET

When you can understand and tap into a new mindset, you will not only create possibilities for yourself but also those around you. To discover how to free your mindset, think about the following:

Individually:

- Reflect on deeply held assumptions; ask yourself, What if the opposite were true?

- Seek out diverse perspectives and listen without judgment.

- Challenge your automatic thoughts and habitual patterns, where did they come from?

- Expose yourself to new environments, people, or ideas regularly.

- Embrace uncertainty and let go of the need for immediate answers.

- Keep a "beginner's mind" approach to every situation, as if seeing it for the first time.

- Replace "I know" with "I'm curious."

- Journal or meditate to increase awareness of thought patterns and biases.

As a leader:

- Reexamine how you define success, are your measures outdated?

- Ask, Where am I limiting my team by thinking too narrowly?

- Observe how you respond to new or unconventional ideas: do you encourage or shut them down?

- Lead experiments, try new approaches, evaluate results, and learn.

- Make time to think, not just do; leadership requires mental space.

CALLING FOR CHANGE

While sustainability efforts often focus on fashion, energy, and food, the tech industry, especially smartphones, remains a major, overlooked contributor to environmental harm. Devices are designed with short lifespans and built-in obsolescence, pushing consumers to upgrade every few years just to maintain performance or battery life. This upgrade culture generates massive e-waste and wastes valuable resources, all while boosting profits for tech companies that benefit from the constant demand for new products.

The environmental and human cost of this model is staggering. But one company is challenging the status quo: Fairphone. In an industry where the norm is replacement rather than upgrades,

Fairphone represents a radical shift in thinking. Instead of following the industry's profit-driven norms, Fairphone freed their mindset and reimagined what a smartphone could be—ethical, repairable, and sustainable. Their phones are designed to last, with modular parts that users can easily replace, like the battery or camera, extending the device's life and reducing waste.

Fairphone's innovation goes beyond hardware. They source materials ethically, ensure fair labor, and promote transparency throughout their supply chain. They aren't just making a better product, they're reshaping the values that define the tech industry. While others see consumers, Fairphone sees people. While others see waste, they see opportunity.

At its heart, Fairphone's mission is about mindset. They questioned the invisible rules of the industry and built something different. In doing so, they proved that freeing your mindset isn't just radical, it's necessary. Because real change doesn't start with a product. It starts with the courage to ask: *Why not do it differently?*

Fairphone models that freeing your mindset is the most important thing you can do. It means refusing to live life by someone else's rules, especially the invisible ones. The ones that sound like:

- "That's just how it is."

- "People like us don't do things like that."

- "Be realistic."

- "No one else has done it before."

These statements aren't facts. They're fences. And freeing your mindset means tearing them down.

Freeing your mindset isn't just radical, it's necessary.

CONNECTING THE UNCONNECTED

During the 1971 Liberation War in Bangladesh, a young boy was sent to fetch medicine for his sick brother. The nearest doctor was more than 7 miles away. After walking the long distance, he found the doctor wasn't there. That boy, Iqbal Quadir, wouldn't know it then, but this moment would one day shape the future of his country.

Decades later, while working in the United States, Iqbal reflected on how easily people could communicate across distances. He realized that access to communication, so vital for healthcare, education, and opportunity, was still out of reach for millions in rural Bangladesh. In 1993, the average Bangladeshi earned about $340 a year, while a mobile phone cost $500 to manufacture. Making mobile communication accessible seemed impossible.

But Iqbal refused to accept that. He freed his mindset and challenged the assumption that mobile phones were only for the wealthy and envisioned them as tools for empowerment. What if people could pay for phones gradually, using them to earn income and lift themselves out of poverty? That shift in thinking became the foundation of his bold idea.

He partnered with Grameen Bank, known for pioneering micro-finance, and after years of persistence, launched Grameenphone in 1997. By combining mobile technology with microloans, Iqbal helped bring affordable communication to millions. Suddenly, rural communities had access to information, markets, and services that had long been out of reach.

Iqbal's innovation didn't just connect people, it transformed mindsets. He saw that development didn't need to come from the top down; it could rise from the people themselves. His belief that connectivity was a *right*, not a luxury, helped lift millions out of poverty and reshaped Bangladesh's economy. Grameenphone became one of the country's largest telecom providers and a global model for inclusive innovation.

To free your mindset is to stop waiting for permission, to realize that the world as we know it was built by people, and it can be rebuilt by you. That's what made Iqbal astonishing: not just his solution, but the belief behind it.

PEANUTS AND POSSIBILITY

In global health, freeing your mindset often means challenging deeply held assumptions about how care must be delivered. One powerful example comes from efforts to treat childhood malnutrition. For years, the standard approach required hospital-based inpatient treatment, often out of reach for families in rural or resource-limited settings. This model, while well-intentioned, created barriers that limited access and left many children untreated.

To free your mindset is to stop waiting for permission, to realize that the world as we know it was built by people, and it can be rebuilt by you.

A team at Project Peanut Butter broke the convention by asking transformative questions: *What if we could treat severe acute malnutrition at home? What if we could reach more children?* This led to the development of Ready-to-Use Therapeutic Foods (RUTFs), nutrient-rich, peanut-based pastes that caregivers could administer themselves. By shifting treatment from hospitals to communities, they enabled faster, more widespread access to lifesaving care, dramatically improving survival rates.

This mindset shift exemplifies the essence of innovation in global health—challenging what's always been done, trusting local capacity, and designing solutions that fit the realities on the ground. By empowering families instead of relying solely on formal health systems, and by leveraging local ingredients to keep costs low, this approach redefined what effective pediatric care could look like. Freeing your mindset, in this case, unlocked a scalable, dignified, and culturally appropriate model of care.

AS A LEADER, HOW DO YOU HELP OTHERS DISCOVER AND TAP INTO A FREE MINDSET?

As a leader, helping others discover and tap into a free mindset begins with encouraging, questioning, and rewarding those who respectfully challenge assumptions. It's important to normalize failure as an essential part of exploration and innovation, creating an environment where learning is valued over perfection. Share stories of your own mindset shifts, instances where changing your perspective led to meaningful breakthroughs, as these examples show that growth often comes from rethinking long-held beliefs.

Diversifying teams by bringing together individuals with contrasting experiences and voices naturally invites broader thinking and fresh ideas. You can also facilitate idea labs, learning sessions, or thought exercises designed to push boundaries and open new mental pathways. To truly unlock a team's thinking, leaders must remove the fear of being wrong; people are far more likely to explore openly when they feel psychologically safe.

Encourage your team to replace statements such as "We've always done it this way," with forward-thinking questions such as "What's possible now?" And perhaps most importantly, model vulnerability, admit when your own thinking was limited, and show how you grew as a result. Your transparency will inspire others to do the same.

ADDING UP THE PRINCIPLES

Fueling your fire, your passion, is essential for freeing your mindset because it becomes the inner force that burns through doubt, fear, and limitations. When you're deeply connected to what lights you up, you stop asking for permission and start finding possibilities.

Passion is what kept Arunachalam Muruganantham experimenting with sanitary pads even when the world laughed at him, what kept Iqbal Quadir chasing the vision of rural connectivity despite impossible economics, and what drove Fairphone to challenge an entire industry.

Passion gives you the stamina to push past "how things have always been" and imagine what could be. It makes freeing your mindset not just an idea, but a mission you're willing to fight for.

Passion doesn't just break boundaries, it builds belief. And that belief becomes the bridge between vision and action, between the ordinary and the astonishing.

HOW TO FREE YOUR MINDSET

Freeing your mindset means questioning the limits you've accepted as facts and daring to imagine something radically better. It's the shift from "That's just how it is," to "What if it could be different?" When you free your mindset, you stop playing by outdated rules and start designing your own path.

The following are six steps to take toward freeing your mindset and living an astonishing life:

1. Question What "Normal" Really Means

What are you accepting as a given? What's "just how it is" that actually *shouldn't* be? When something feels off, even if it's accepted by everyone around you, that's your cue to dig deeper. Ask: *Who benefits from this staying the same? Who suffers?*

> Arunachalam Muruganantham questioned why menstruation had to be taboo and why women couldn't access basic hygiene products.

2. Flip the Frame

Instead of asking, *"Can I do this?"* ask, *"What would need to be true for this to work?"* Freeing your mindset means redefining the problem so a new solution can emerge.

> Iqbal Quadir didn't accept that mobile phones were a luxury for the rich. He flipped the frame: What if phones could make people richer?

3. Stop Waiting for Permission

If you wait for consensus or a clear path, you'll wait forever. Move before you're ready. Innovators don't follow signs, they paint their own.

> No one gave Fairphone approval to redesign the entire tech industry. They just started.

4. Make Yourself Uncomfortable on Purpose

Change begins at the edge of discomfort. If your ideas don't scare you, or others, they're probably not big enough.

Muruganantham was mocked, abandoned, and even labeled mentally unstable. But he kept going, because once your mindset is free, the noise can't hold you back.

5. Prototype Possibility

Don't just imagine better, *build* better. Try something small. Test your vision in the real world. Your mindset isn't truly free until you take action based on the new truths you've claimed.

Charlie Jeffers created a scalable program moving from his neighborhood to distributing LEGO sets to children around the world.

6. Refuse to Go Back

Once you've seen what's possible, don't let the world drag you back to "realistic." Freeing your mindset is not a one-time decision. It's a daily practice of reminding yourself: *The world is changeable. So am I.*

Project Peanut Butter not only revolutionized treatment for acute malnutrition but also continued to think creatively through their local production, caring for mothers who are malnourished, and developing compostable packaging. They refused to stop after addressing one idea, pushing the boundaries in multiple dimensions.

BRINGING IT TOGETHER

The most astonishing lives aren't built on luck or perfection, they're built on the courage to think differently. When you free your mindset, you stop living by default and start living by design. You see limits as invitations. Obstacles as raw material. And doubt? That becomes the spark, not the end.

People who free their mindset don't wait for permission to think in new ways, they let their questions reshape the world. They challenge what is "normal" and show us what's possible when vision outpaces fear. Freeing your mindset doesn't mean never being afraid. It means refusing to be ruled by what you've been told is impossible.

So ask yourself: What belief am I still holding on to that's keeping me less than my best? What rule am I ready to rewrite?

To be astonishing, you don't need to have all the answers. You just need to believe that there's more than one way, and the boldness to follow it.

Chapter 5

OUTWORK YOUR ORDINARY

The difference between ordinary and astonishing often comes down to one simple yet powerful principle: outwork your ordinary. It's easy to get comfortable, to settle into a rhythm that feels safe, predictable, and manageable. But greatness isn't built on comfort. It's built on pushing beyond what's expected, challenging yourself to do more, be more, and stay relentless in the pursuit of your goals. How you do everything matters.

Outworking your ordinary isn't about perfection. It's about putting in the hard work when no one is watching, knowing that small efforts compound over time. When you outwork your ordinary, you don't just *expect* things to happen, you *make* them happen through relentless action.

What does it mean to outwork your ordinary? Outworking your ordinary doesn't just mean longer hours. It means better focus, deeper intention, and a commitment to doing the work that actually moves you forward. It's not about burnout, it's about breakthrough. You're not competing with others. You're challenging yesterday's version of yourself. It's not about a single moment of brilliance, but about a sustained effort over time.

Success doesn't belong to those who wait for the perfect conditions, it belongs to those who are willing to work for it, no matter how difficult the journey may be. It means pushing through the days when you feel like giving up. It means showing up even when it's hard. It means doing what others are unwilling to do, whether learning new skills, staying up late to get ahead, or facing challenges head-on instead of avoiding them. It may be about changing how you see the challenges or how you usually solve the problems. It's about finding a way when there seems to be no way and refusing to let obstacles define your journey.

Ordinary is average. Anyone can do average. People who out-work their ordinary are anything but average. They are astonishing,

Success doesn't belong to those who wait for the perfect conditions, it belongs to those who are willing to work for it, no matter how difficult the journey may be.

Ordinary is average. Anyone can do average.

and they achieve astonishing results. We all know someone who had talent but stopped short. They had the idea, the opportunity, even the advantage, but they never followed through. They waited for the "right time," coasted on potential, or let fear hold the reins. That's what happens when you stay comfortable, you shrink your possibilities.

Astonishing never lives in the comfort zone.

When you commit to outworking your ordinary, you unlock your true potential. You give yourself the freedom to evolve, to grow, and to become the version of yourself you once thought impossible. The power to create something extraordinary lies within you, and the key to unlocking that potential is simple: work harder, push further, and believe in the power of your own relentless effort.

THE POWER OF PRESENCE

One story of astonishing character comes to mind from my (AS) time working at a children's hospital in Memphis, Tennessee. In the corner room of the Cardiac Intensive Care Unit was a young boy who spent many months hospitalized due to congenital heart disease. He was incredibly sick and medically fragile. One day, he experienced a cardiac arrest, and a full resuscitation ensued, including CPR. The mom wasn't at the bedside but was called and quickly arrived.

When she did, the Environmental Services worker was there waiting for her. The EVS worker had stopped her daily responsibility of helping keep the hospital clean and safe to ensure she was present and could stand with the mom during one of the most unimaginably difficult times a parent would ever face. Her arm wrapped around the mom as the remainder of the medical team focused on caring for the young child.

This EVS worker was astonishing, not because it was in her job description to provide care and comfort, not because anyone asked her to be there, but because she chose to outwork her ordinary. She understood, perhaps more deeply than most, that in moments of crisis, the smallest gestures can carry the greatest weight. She didn't just see a task list that day, she saw a human being in need of presence, of compassion, of strength. And she showed up.

There were world-class physicians in that room. Nurses who were operating at the highest level of precision and skill. Alarms, monitors, protocols, all essential. But it was the quiet, grounding presence of someone whose job typically goes unnoticed that transformed that moment. She didn't perform a medical miracle. She didn't change the clinical outcome. But she made sure that mother wasn't alone. And that is no small feat.

To be astonishing doesn't always mean being the loudest voice or holding the highest title. Sometimes, it means seeing beyond what's expected and showing up when it matters most. Outwork your ordinary means refusing to let your role define your reach. It's the daily decision to bring your full humanity to the work, no matter what that work is.

Outwork your ordinary means refusing to let your role define your reach.

That day, in that corner room of the CICU, excellence wasn't just measured in heartbeats recovered or procedures completed, it was also found in the heartbeat of empathy, in the extraordinary compassion of an ordinary worker who dared to rise above routine. She didn't need recognition. She didn't need applause. She simply lived the kind of astonishing that changes everything.

SADDLE UP

Dave Munson didn't set out to create just another leather bag. When he started Saddleback Leather in 2003, he set out to outwork the ordinary, to craft something so enduring, so uncompromising in quality, that it would outlive its owner. His now-iconic motto says it all: *"They'll fight over it when you're dead."* That mindset, building with the end in mind, didn't just create exceptional products, it shaped a company that does everything the hard way…because the hard way is usually the right way.

The hard way is usually the right way.

Saddleback's leather backpacks and bags are not designed for trends or shortcuts. Dave and his team use only the toughest full-grain leather, pigskin lining, and the strongest threads and hardware they can find. No zippers. No cheap components. Nothing breakable. Just obsessive attention to durability, function, and legacy. Saddleback leather bags, backpacks, and briefcases are some of the best-designed and undoubtedly the longest-lasting in the industry. The company even offers a 100-year warranty, because mediocrity has no place in their mission.

Dave's products and customer service are truly astonishing, but he didn't stop at making the best leather bags on earth. Alongside his wife Suzette, Dave founded Love 41, a sister company (or "wife-company" as Dave affectionately calls it) that uses its profits to change lives. Love 41 is committed to loving and lifting orphans, single moms, and ex-prisoners by giving them opportunity, dignity, and purpose.

They work with communities and families globally and have engaged in projects such as providing free daycare for those attending training for sewing or beauty school in Rwanda, starting a school in Mexico, and providing scholarships for education for children in need. They leave a lasting influence on everyone involved. It's not charity, it's transformation built into the business model.

Dave Munson and his team exemplify what it means to outwork your ordinary. They pour excellence into their craft and love into their mission. They didn't just build a company, they built a movement. And that's what astonishing people do: they refuse to settle, they work harder than necessary, and they link their talent to a purpose greater than themselves.

TAPPING INTO OUTWORKING YOUR ORDINARY

When you can understand and tap into a level of performance beyond the normal, you will not only create possibilities for yourself but also those around you. To discover how to outwork your ordinary, think about the following:

Individually:

- Clarify your goals, define what success looks like beyond mediocrity.

- Identify your "why"; when effort is tied to purpose, it becomes sustainable.

- Analyze your habits: what's average, and what could be optimized?

- Study people who consistently outperform and reverse-engineer their effort.

- Schedule discipline; hard work isn't spontaneous, it's structured.

- Reflect on past wins; what did it take, and are you willing to do it again?

As a leader:

- Ask yourself, *Where am I settling for average?*

- Set a personal standard higher than external expectations.

- Find your grind rhythm: when do you perform best, and how can you leverage that?

- Track your inputs, not just outcomes—what you put in determines what you get out.

FROM PANTYHOSE TO POWERHOUSE

Many people struggle to find their path. Even when they land on a great idea, success doesn't come easily, it takes persistence, hard work,

Astonishing people link their talent to a purpose greater than themselves.

and the grit to keep going when things get tough. That kind of effort, of outworking your ordinary, is exactly what defines Sara Blakely's story.

After college, Sara didn't have a dream job. She worked at Disney, sold fax machines door-to-door, and kept searching for something that sparked passion. One night, frustrated with how her clothes fit, she cut the feet off her pantyhose to create a smoother look under her outfit. The result was simple but powerful: a more comfortable, invisible kind of shapewear. She had no fashion or business background, just a gut feeling that she was onto something big. But an idea, even a brilliant one, means nothing without follow-through.

With only $5,000 in savings, she worked by day as a sales trainer and built her idea by night. She cold-called factories, taught herself the industry, and wrote her own patent. Dozens told her no. She kept going. Eventually, she found a factory that said yes and she launched her company, Spanx.

Her big break came when Oprah featured Spanx on her show in 2000, sending sales through the roof. But it wasn't luck, it was years of behind-the-scenes hustle. Sara became the face of Spanx, showing

An idea, even a brilliant one, means nothing without follow-through.

up on talk shows, doing her own PR, and using every opportunity to share her story. She even appeared on *Rebel Billionaire*, winning $750,000 from Richard Branson, which she used to launch the Sara Blakely Foundation, supporting female entrepreneurs around the world. Spanx became a billion-dollar brand. And Sara became one of the first self-made female billionaires.

Sara Blakely didn't succeed because of a single moment of inspiration, she succeeded because she *outworked her ordinary* every step of the way. She turned scissors and an idea into a billion-dollar brand through relentless effort, self-belief, and resilience.

TRAJECTORY OF TENACITY

Few have outworked their ordinary quite like Katherine Johnson, a pioneering NASA mathematician whose calculations were critical to some of the most significant space missions in history.

Born in 1918 in segregated West Virginia, Katherine's extraordinary gift for mathematics revealed itself from a young age. Despite systemic barriers of race and gender, she relentlessly pursued education, graduating from college at 18.

She went on to work at NASA (then NACA), where she was instrumental in calculating the trajectory for Alan Shepard's first American spaceflight, the orbital flight of John Glenn, and the Apollo 11 moon landing. Glenn himself refused to fly a groundbreaking mission unless Johnson personally verified the flight path.

Katherine worked long hours, often behind the scenes, performing calculations by hand before computers were widely trusted. Her precision and dedication weren't just a job, they were life-or-death contributions to the space race.

Katherine persisted in a world that rarely recognized women of color in science. Day after day, she showed up with relentless precision and a determination to be indispensable, not just excellent. She didn't just do what was asked, she rose above, driven by a deep commitment to others and the larger purpose of exploration and progress.

AS A LEADER, HOW DO YOU HELP OTHERS OUTWORK THE ORDINARY?

As a leader, helping others outwork their ordinary starts with setting high expectations while offering high levels of support. People are more likely to rise to the challenge when they know they're not doing it alone. Make it a habit to celebrate effort, not just outcomes, by honoring the process and recognizing the grind that leads to growth.

Be transparent about the hidden work behind your own success to normalize the level of dedication it takes to achieve excellence. Coach team members to define what "ordinary" looks like for them, and then challenge them to go beyond it. Partnerships can be powerful tools for sustaining consistent effort, offering both encouragement and responsibility.

Foster a culture where hard work is not only accepted but respected; make it clear that going above and beyond is part of what it means to be part of your organization. Empower people to take ownership of their results and the work ethic that gets them there.

Finally, actively identify and remove distractions, friction points, or excuses that may be blocking their ability to perform at their best. When people know their hard work matters and is supported, they are far more likely to give their best consistently.

ADDING UP THE PRINCIPLES

Fuel your fire is essential for outworking your ordinary because it sustains your energy, resilience, and focus when things get hard, which they inevitably will. Passion isn't just about excitement, it's what keeps you going when results are slow, when rejection stings, and when effort outweighs reward. When your inner fire is lit by purpose, vision, or belief in your idea, you're not just grinding through tasks, you're pushing past limits. That fire is what turns routine into resolve, and persistence into progress. It keeps you moving when there's no applause, no road map, and no guarantee. And over time, it transforms ordinary effort into extraordinary impact.

Free your mindset is crucial for outworking your ordinary because it breaks the mental limits that keep you stuck in what's comfortable or expected. When you let go of fear, doubt, or rigid beliefs about what's possible, you open yourself to bold ideas, unconventional paths, and a deeper capacity for growth. A free mindset doesn't wait for permission, it experiments, adapts, and sees obstacles as challenges to rise above. Without that freedom, you'll work hard, but likely stay within the boundaries of "ordinary." With it, you unlock your potential to become truly astonishing.

Outwork your ordinary is what allows you to reimagine not only what you do, but who you can become. Because before you do anything extraordinary, you have to believe it's possible.

HOW TO OUTWORK YOUR ORDINARY

Outwork your ordinary means refusing to settle for average effort, average outcomes, or average thinking. It's pushing past comfort, questioning what you've been told is "enough," and committing to do more than what's required. It's the mindset shift from "This is good enough," to "How far can I take this?"

The following are six steps to take toward outworking your ordinary and living an astonishing life:

1. Set a Higher Standard Than What's Expected

Don't just meet the baseline, exceed it. Ordinary stops at "good enough." Astonishing pushes for excellence even when no one's watching.

> Saddleback Leather models this with their incomparable product and 100-year warranty, highlighting their belief in the work they're doing.

2. Fuel Your Fire Daily

Connect with your "why." Passion won't sustain itself, feed it with purpose, reflection, and reminders of what matters most.

> Sara Blakely continually tapped into the passion behind her product in order to lead it to the success it has found today.

3. Refuse to Let Your Role Define Your Impact

Titles don't limit greatness. Bring excellence to every corner of your work, whether you're leading the meeting or cleaning the floors.

> Think back to the EVS worker who stopped what she was doing to comfort a scared mother.

4. Turn Setbacks Into Fuel

Expect resistance, failure, and rejection, and use them to sharpen your resolve. The ordinary quit. The astonishing adapt and advance.

> Rather than let the systemic obstacles diminish her, Katherine Johnson used them as fuel to work through and prove that brilliance knows no gender or color.

5. "Did I do anything today that pushed past ordinary?"

Ask yourself this at the end of each day. If the answer is yes, even in a small way, you're building momentum. If the answer is no, don't judge, just recommit.

> Astonishing lives in daily decisions, the EVS worker certainly lived this that day in the Cardiac Intensive Care Unit.

6. Stay Humble, Stay Hungry

No matter how much progress you've made, never stop learning, improving, or hustling. Ordinary rests. You don't.

> Sara Blakely challenged herself to learn and grow at each phase of running a brand-new company.

BRINGING IT TOGETHER

Outworking your ordinary isn't about being superhuman, it's about being *fully human* in a world that often settles for less. It's the daily decision to show up with purpose, to stretch beyond comfort, and to act with relentless intention. Whether you're building a billion-dollar company from a dorm room idea, supporting a grieving parent in a hospital hallway, or crafting a product with obsessive care, your commitment to excellence becomes the difference-maker.

This chapter isn't just about hustle, it's about heart. It's about rejecting mediocrity and embracing the mindset that every interaction, every effort, and every challenge is an opportunity to go beyond what's expected. When you outwork your ordinary, you don't just change your results, you change your identity. You become someone who inspires, who elevates, who astonishes.

And the beautiful truth? Anyone can do it. No matter your background, title, or starting point, extraordinary is available to those willing to put in extraordinary effort. So today, don't just show up— show up astonishing.

Chapter 6

FORGE YOUR RESILIENCE

Forging your resilience is at the heart of what it means to be an astonishing human being. Life doesn't always go as planned; we all face failures, setbacks, and roadblocks. These moments don't define us by the outcome they produce; instead, they shape the beliefs we carry about ourselves. Too often, we confuse temporary failure with permanent limitation, letting challenges convince us we're incapable. But resilience is the act of standing up again and choosing what we believe in despite what's gone wrong.

Resilience is your ability to recover from adversity, setbacks, and challenges. We must cultivate a growth mindset to view challenges as opportunities, shifting from a fixed mindset to one of possibility and potential. With this perspective, setbacks can become stepping stones to success.

Patience plays a quiet yet powerful role in this process. True resilience isn't just about bouncing back quickly, it's about enduring the slow, sometimes painful journey of growth. Being astonishing doesn't require perfection; it requires persistence, self-compassion, and the patience to let time do its work. Life will happen. The question is, how will you respond when it does?

Setbacks can become stepping stones to success.

WARRIOR BEYOND THE SCREEN

Few people have forged their resilience quite like Chadwick Boseman. When it was announced that he would play *Black Panther*, the first Black superhero in mainstream comics to lead a major film, it marked a historic moment in cinema. But Boseman's casting wasn't just about filling a superhero role. It was about placing someone extraordinary in it. Known for portraying real-life icons including Jackie Robinson, James Brown, and Thurgood Marshall, Boseman brought a deep sense of authenticity, dignity, and power to every role he played. As T'Challa, he inspired millions.

While audiences celebrated the justice he fought for on-screen, few knew about the battles he fought off-screen.

Born in 1976, Boseman's rise was far from easy. He studied acting and directing at Howard University, but his journey was shaped by financial hardship and a lack of connections. When he was accepted into the British American Drama Academy's prestigious Midsummer program, he couldn't afford to attend, until Denzel Washington stepped in and quietly paid the tuition for his class. That single act of generosity would deeply influence Boseman, who often spoke about how it inspired him to one day give back the same way.

As his career soared, Boseman made good on that promise. He mentored young artists, funded scholarships for Black students, and supported health initiatives, especially those focused on cancer care in underserved communities. His success became a platform for others.

What made Boseman's story even more remarkable was the quiet courage with which he faced his greatest personal challenge. In 2016, he was diagnosed with colon cancer. He told no one outside of his closest circle. While undergoing multiple surgeries and treatments, he continued to perform in physically and emotionally demanding roles. He starred in *Black Panther, Da 5 Bloods, 21 Bridges, Marshall,* and *Ma Rainey's Black Bottom,* all while silently fighting for his life.

Being astonishing doesn't require perfection; it requires persistence, self-compassion, and the patience to let time do its work.

When Boseman's death was announced in 2020, the world was stunned. No one had known. In his silence, there was strength. In his struggle, there was purpose. And in his performances, there was a depth that came from real pain and perseverance.

Chadwick Boseman's legacy is not just about the roles he played. It's about the resilience he lived. He taught the world that greatness doesn't always come from loud victories, it often comes from quiet determination. His life is a testament to what it means to live with purpose, grace, and authenticity, even in the face of overwhelming adversity. Boseman serves as a powerful inspiration, reminding us that resilience isn't just about momentary strength. True resilience lies in continuously rising with unwavering determination, purpose, and grace, no matter the challenge.

Boseman also teaches us that resilience drives long-term success. This resilience takes many forms: emotional, physical, mental,

---

True resilience lies in continuously rising with unwavering determination, purpose, and grace, no matter the challenge.

---

social, and even spiritual. *Emotional* resilience helps us navigate loss, failure, and disappointment by managing emotions and confronting fears. *Physical* resilience enhances energy, focus, and stamina, while *mental* resilience allows us to stay clear-headed, adaptable, and calm under pressure. *Social* resilience relies on strong relationships, communication, and collaboration, especially in difficult times. *Spiritual* resilience provides strength and purpose through personal beliefs. Together, these forms of resilience shape our ability to overcome adversity and thrive.

BUILT TO BOUNCE BACK

Embracing failure as a stepping stone to success is key to building resilience. Failure is not the opposite of success—it's a necessary part of the journey. It serves as a learning experience for what is yet to come. History is full of individuals who faced setbacks before achieving greatness, proving that perseverance through failure fosters growth.

Thomas Edison may be one of the most famous examples of resilience in the face of repeated failures. Edison is known for inventing the modern lightbulb, but he failed more than 1,000 times before getting it right. When asked about his repeated failures, he famously said, "I have not failed. I've just found 10,000 ways that won't work."

Beyond the lightbulb, Edison faced challenges in his early life. He was expelled from school because his teachers thought he was "too slow" to learn. He also failed multiple times as an entrepreneur, including an electric vote recorder that nobody wanted and early

---

Failure is not the opposite of success—it's a necessary part of the journey.

---

ventures that went bankrupt. However, his persistence led to more than 1,000 patents and the creation of General Electric (GE), one of the most successful companies in history.

Thomas Edison's story exemplifies resilience through his unwavering determination despite repeated failures. Instead of seeing setbacks as defeats, he viewed them as learning opportunities, stating that each failure brought him closer to success. His persistence in the face of over 1,000 failed attempts ultimately led to one of the greatest inventions in history, proving that resilience is key to achieving breakthroughs. Thomas Edison is astonishing because of his incredible contributions to technology and innovation as a prolific inventor, revolutionizing daily life.

We might also think of the *Chicken Soup for the Soul* series of books. The authors, Jack Canfield and Mark Victor Hansen, contacted 144 publishers before they found one willing to take on the project. This series of books has gone on to sell more than 500 million copies worldwide. Or of Michael Jordan, who was cut from his high school basketball team but used that failure to fuel his legendary career. The list continues… Time after time, if you talk to astonishing people and leaders of astonishing organizations, they will tell you of initial failures and setbacks. They had to forge their resilience to succeed.

Beyond overcoming obstacles, resilience is also nurtured through everyday habits. Small, consistent actions, like yoga, meditation, journaling, or simply showing up when things feel difficult, help build long-term strength. Prioritizing self-care and allowing time to recharge are just as essential in maintaining resilience as pushing forward through challenges.

Simone Biles is astonishing because she redefined what it means to be strong, not just by winning medals, but by knowing when to step back. At the peak of global competition, she made the bold decision to prioritize her mental health, challenging the world's expectations of toughness. In doing so, she gave permission to millions to value their well-being over performance. Her courage to speak openly and act protectively for herself transformed the conversation around resilience, strength, and self-worth.

TAPPING INTO YOUR RESILIENCE

When you can understand and tap into your resilience, you will not only create possibilities for yourself, but also those around you. To discover how to forge your resilience, think about the following:

Individually:

- Reflect on past setbacks: what did you learn, and how did you grow?

- Build habits that promote emotional regulation (exercise, rest, mindfulness).

- Focus on what you can control, not what you cannot.

- Redefine failure as a building block, not a dead end.

- Develop a personal mantra or values that ground you during adversity.

- Seek out small challenges intentionally to build your resilience skills.

As a leader:

- Acknowledge your scars; resilience comes from real struggle, not theory.

- Identify your personal response pattern to adversity: fight, flight, freeze?

- Ask, *Where am I modeling bounce-back for my team, and where am I hiding it?*

- Reframe pressure as a proving ground for growth.

TURNING SETBACKS INTO STREAMS

Resilience is not just a personal trait, it's embedded within the DNA of successful organizations. Organizations demonstrate resilience by adapting to challenges, maintaining a long-term vision, and fostering a culture of innovation. They do this by investing in flexible strategies, diversifying revenue streams, and learning from failures to continuously improve.

Netflix is a powerful example of a company that forged its resilience through risk, reinvention, and relentless perseverance. Today, it's hard to imagine daily life without Netflix; millions of people stream movies and shows from their homes instead of going to theaters. But this level of influence didn't happen overnight, and it certainly wasn't without setbacks. Netflix's success is the result of bold decisions, painful losses, and a willingness to evolve.

In the late 1990s, home entertainment was dominated by DVD rentals, and Blockbuster was the undisputed leader, with stores on nearly every corner. It was during this time that Reed Hastings and Marc Randolph launched a small startup called Netflix. Their idea? An online DVD rental service with no late fees, operating on a subscription model. At the time, it seemed like a long shot, an underdog attempt to challenge a giant.

But Netflix's model caught on. For $17.99 a month, customers could rent up to three DVDs at a time from a vast catalog, keeping them as long as they wanted with no penalties. This was a radical shift in convenience and customer experience.

Still, taking on Blockbuster was no easy task. By 2001, Netflix had only 300,000 subscribers and was losing over $50 million a year. Physical rentals still ruled, and profitability seemed far off. In a last-ditch effort, Hastings and Randolph offered to sell Netflix to Blockbuster for $50 million. Their pitch was straightforward: Blockbuster could handle the in-store business, and Netflix would manage the online side. Together, they could dominate both worlds.

Blockbuster's CEO, John Antioco, famously laughed them out of the room.

Most startups would have folded. Being dismissed by the industry leader could easily have crushed their momentum. But Netflix didn't back down. Instead, they doubled down on their vision. They recognized that the future of entertainment wasn't in physical rentals, it was in streaming. So they pivoted, investing heavily in building a digital platform and licensing content.

The rest is history. Netflix went on to revolutionize the entertainment industry, becoming a global streaming giant with millions of subscribers around the world. Blockbuster, unwilling to adapt, filed for bankruptcy and faded into history.

Netflix's story is about more than just market disruption, it's a master class in resilience. They didn't just survive rejection and loss; they transformed those moments into fuel for innovation. Where others saw dead ends, Netflix saw new beginnings.

And in a twist of irony, years later, a comedy series titled *Blockbuster* premiered on Netflix. A quiet nod to the very company that once refused to see their potential.

Similar to Netflix, what follows is a list of how well-known and astonishing companies have forged their resilience as part of their journey.

Apple (1990s-early 2000s) – Apple was on the verge of bankruptcy in 1997, struggling with low sales and poor leadership decisions. Microsoft even invested $150 million to keep it afloat. Steve Jobs' return and the launch of the iMac, iPod, and later the iPhone turned Apple into one of the most valuable and profitable companies in the world.

Airbnb (2008) – The founders of Airbnb resorted to selling cereal boxes just to keep their startup afloat. They struggled to gain investors, but after refining their platform and receiving funding, Airbnb became a global travel disruptor.

Starbucks (1980s & 2008) – In the early days, Starbucks was just a small coffee shop chain. Howard Schultz bought the company and struggled to expand. Later, during the 2008 financial crisis, Starbucks had to close hundreds of stores and rework its strategy. It rebounded by refocusing on customer experience and digital innovations like mobile ordering.

LEGO (2003-2004) – LEGO was nearly bankrupt in the early 2000s due to bad business decisions, such as overexpanding into video games and theme parks. After refocusing on its core products (brick sets) and launching collaborations like LEGO Star Wars, the company bounced back to become one of the most valuable toy brands in the world.

Nike (1970s & 1980s) – Nike struggled in its early years, with cash flow problems and competition from Adidas. At one point, the company couldn't even afford advertising. The breakthrough came with the signing of Michael Jordan in the 1980s, which launched the Air Jordan brand and turned Nike into a global powerhouse.

This list could extend endlessly. Strong leadership, employee support, and the ability to pivot in response to crises, such as economic downturns or technological disruptions, help organizations withstand adversity and emerge stronger. Poignantly, each organization's ability to recover from obstacles, invest in long-term growth, and continuously reinvent themselves highlights why resilience is a key factor in sustained success. These organizations are global leaders in their respective industry and are astonishing in their own ways.

AS A LEADER, HOW DO YOU HELP OTHERS FORGE THEIR RESILIENCE?

As a leader, helping others forge their resilience begins by normalizing setbacks and openly sharing your own experiences, including what happened next and how you grew. When people see that challenges are part of the journey, not the end of it, they begin to view adversity differently.

Create intentional space for your team to process difficulties, reflect on what happened, and extract meaningful lessons. Actively highlight moments when resilience has shown up within the

When people see that challenges are part of the journey, not the end of it, they begin to view adversity differently.

organization and use those stories to reinforce that strength comes from struggle. Provide practical tools such as mental fitness training, stress management resources, or coaching to help individuals build their inner capacity to bounce forward.

Make reflection part of your culture by consistently asking questions like, "What did this teach us?" to turn every experience into a growth opportunity. Reinforce the value of persistence by reminding your team that not everything needs to be fast or easy, what matters most is sticking with what's meaningful.

And finally, build psychological safety; people are far more willing to stretch, fail, and try again when they know they won't be judged. Resilience thrives in environments where people feel seen, supported, and trusted.

ADDING UP THE PRINCIPLES

Fueling your fire and finding passion is crucial for resilience because it provides a deep sense of purpose, which can help you stay motivated during tough times. Passion acts as a driving force, helping you overcome obstacles and setbacks by keeping your focus on meaningful goals. When challenges arise, having something you are passionate about gives you the energy and determination to persevere, even when things seem difficult. Passion fosters creativity and problem-solving, allowing you to approach challenges with a sense of curiosity rather than defeat. It transforms setbacks into opportunities for growth, helping you reframe difficulties as part of the journey rather than roadblocks. When resilience is rooted in passion, the process of pushing forward becomes more than just endurance, it becomes a purposeful pursuit that fuels personal and professional fulfillment.

Freeing your mindset and breaking through limitations is essential for resilience because it allows you to view challenges as opportunities rather than obstacles. By shifting your perspective and letting go of self-imposed constraints, you open yourself to new possibilities and growth. This mindset shift enables you to bounce back from setbacks with greater flexibility, creativity, and determination to move forward. When you cultivate a growth-oriented mindset, failures become lessons, and difficulties become stepping stones toward success. Resilience thrives when you embrace change, take risks, and challenge limiting beliefs that hold you back.

Outworking your ordinary is key to resilience because it demonstrates dedication and perseverance, even when faced with setbacks. Progress is earned through consistent effort rather than instant success. By consistently pushing beyond the minimum, you build mental and physical endurance, which strengthens your ability to overcome challenges. This relentless commitment to effort allows you to transform difficulties into opportunities for growth and success, setting you apart from the average. Hard work builds resilience by reinforcing the idea that progress is earned through consistent effort rather than instant success. Each challenge becomes a test of character, and every setback becomes a lesson that fuels future achievements. Ultimately, resilience is not just about enduring hardships but about continuously striving for improvement. When you commit to outworking your ordinary, you redefine what is possible for yourself, proving that perseverance and effort pave the way for long-term success.

HOW TO FORGE YOUR RESILIENCE

Resilience isn't about being tough all the time; it's about choosing strength again and again, even when it feels hard. The astonishing individuals and organizations we've explored—Chadwick Boseman, Netflix, Thomas Edison, Simone Biles—each show us that resilience isn't something you're born with. It's something you build. It's not a trait, it's a toolkit.

The following are seven steps to take toward forging your resilience and living an astonishing life:

1. Accept What You Can't Control

You can't control every circumstance, but you can always control your response. Resilience starts with shifting your energy from "why me?" to "what now?" and choosing action over anxiety.

> Chadwick Boseman couldn't change his cancer diagnosis, but he chose to live with purpose and excellence, continuing to inspire through every performance.

2. Feel Fully, Then Move Forward

Being resilient doesn't mean ignoring emotions. It means honoring them, and then rising anyway. Let yourself process pain, fear, or disappointment, and then take the next step.

> Netflix could've let Blockbuster's rejection define them. Instead, they turned that setback into fuel for their future.

3. Stay Connected

Resilient people are not lone wolves. Support systems are the secret weapon—mentors, friends, family, or teams. Connection fuels endurance.

> Chadwick Boseman's connection with Howard University and Denzel Washington didn't just shape his career, it strengthened his spirit. Later, he paid it forward by mentoring others.

4. Practice Optimism, Realistically

Hope is a discipline. It's the belief that things can get better, even if they're hard right now. Reframe setbacks as setups.

> Thomas Edison saw every "failed" attempt as one step closer to success. His optimism was grounded in persistence.

5. Stack Small Wins

Confidence grows through action. Every small step forward is a building block for future strength. Celebrate the effort, not just the outcome.

> Airbnb's founders sold cereal just to survive. Every scrappy win mattered, and built the foundation for a billion-dollar business.

6. Care for Your Body and Mind

Resilience requires energy. Physical and mental stamina come from consistent care, rest, movement, mindfulness, and nourishment.

Simone Biles stepped back at the Olympics to protect her mental health. That decision wasn't weakness, it was wisdom. Real resilience starts with self-respect.

7. Keep Going, No Matter What

The most resilient people are not perfect, they're persistent. They show up, again and again, no matter how tough it gets.

Chicken Soup for the Soul persisted through rejection. Michael Jordan kept training after getting cut. LEGO kept building through bankruptcy. They didn't stop, and neither should you.

BRINGING IT TOGETHER

To be astonishing, you must cultivate resilience, persisting and thriving in the face of life's inevitable obstacles. This is not a trait that some are simply born with; rather, it is a skill, a mindset, and a discipline that must be intentionally developed and fortified over time. Resilience is about rising when you fall, learning from setbacks, and refusing to be defined by challenges. It is about harnessing adversity as fuel for growth and transformation.

Consider Chadwick Boseman, who embodied the very essence of resilience. Despite privately battling a terminal illness, he continued to deliver performances that inspired millions, portraying strength, dignity, and unwavering purpose. His legacy is not just in his art but in his perseverance, his ability to push forward when others might have given up. Boseman's journey reminds us that true greatness is not measured solely by success but by the ability to endure, adapt, and excel despite hardships.

You, too, have the power to cultivate this level of resilience. Each setback you encounter is an opportunity to strengthen your character, sharpen your skills, and reaffirm your commitment to your goals. Approach each challenge with confidence and the unwavering belief in your ability to overcome. Let resilience be the foundation upon which you build an astonishing life, one that inspires and leaves an indelible mark on the world.

Chapter 7

LIVE YOUR AUTHENTICITY

Everyone has a unique greatness within them. The key to tapping into your unique greatness and ultimately what makes you astonishing is authenticity. When you discover and become your best authentic self, no one can replicate what you offer, and you can serve everyone around you at a significantly deeper level.

Authenticity is the alignment between who you truly are and how you show up in the world.

It means being honest with yourself and others, living and leading in a way that reflects your core values, beliefs, and identity—not just what others expect of you. It's about dropping the mask, not performing or pretending, and instead showing up with integrity, vulnerability, and clarity.

Authenticity always starts with understanding your values. When you know, at a deep level, what you believe and how that manifests itself in the actions you take, being authentic becomes natural. When you know and are true to your values, the real you shows up, and people will always like the real you versus the fake one. Being real contributes to building trust and respect.

When you know and live your values, when you are being your authentic self, you grow into a more resilient person, and you are effectively able to face adversity. As we discussed in the previous chapter, forging your resilience is at the heart of what it means to be an astonishing human being. For that to happen, a thorough understanding of your values and how to live authentically is critical.[1]

In a personal sense, authenticity is when your thoughts, words, and actions are consistent with your inner truth. In a leadership or organizational context, it's about creating an environment where people feel safe to be themselves, where transparency, trust, and values drive decisions and culture.

Want it in one sentence? Authenticity is the courage to live your truth, without compromise, in a world full of expectations.

Once we discover how to show up and live our truth, everything changes.

HAPPILY ASTONISHING

It's been a while since we first met Pat Hickman. Pat was the President and CEO of Happy State Bank. Yes, that's a real bank's name. The bank was originally founded in Happy, Texas, and the people who work at the bank and the customers of the bank are all very happy.

Pat took a bank that had one location and $10 million in assets and, 32 years later, built it into a bank with 65 locations and $7.4

---

1. To learn more about identifying your personal or organizational values, check out our free "Values Framework" at www.valuesworksheet.com.

Authenticity is the courage to live your truth, without compromise, in a world full of expectations.

billion in assets. He influenced people and communities in profound ways.

Pat didn't finish college and worked at a bank in Amarillo. He had a simple dream: to run a bank in Canyon, his hometown, just down the road from Amarillo. We could share so many things with you about Pat, but this story alone allows you to understand the kind of person he was and the model his life was for so many people. Here, in Pat's own words, is the true story of how he and his investors bought Happy State Bank.

> Carl Small owned a majority share in the bank we wanted to buy, which was located in Happy, Texas. Carl was meeting regularly with me about the possibility of me buying the bank. He knew I wanted to lead the group that bought his bank, and he knew what kind of bank I wanted to run, and he knew I was out raising money.
>
> Weeks went by. Months went by. Carl and I were getting more and more excited. I finally figured I had enough investors put

together to pull this off. Ideally, we wanted to buy out all the stockholders. We just didn't know yet if we could do that or not. So the first goal was just to buy Carl out. The second goal was to buy our way up to 67 percent. And the third goal was to buy out everybody.

I realized it was about time for me to talk pricing with Carl. My investors said to me, "Okay, for Carl's 60.5 percent, you can pay $750,000. You're on your own. Go make it happen." That was as high as I could go.

Carl and I scheduled a meeting to nail down the numbers, to figure out whether or not this thing was going to happen.

I don't know if anybody ever tried to buy a bank before at the McDonald's located at 34th and Coulter in Amarillo, Texas, but that's where we met to try to seal the deal. We went through all the pleasantries. We talked around the subject for a little bit, and then finally I just said, "Carl, I've never bought a bank before, and I don't know where to start."

And he said, "Well, I've never sold one before."

I said, "Carl, give me a hint, let me know what we're looking at."

"Well," he answered, "I'll tell you. My wife and I talked this over. We want a million dollars. That's our price."

And I just looked at him.

I said, "Carl, I'm not gonna insult you. I think my number is so low, you're not going to want to hear it. And I don't want to do that. We're so far apart. Let's just shake hands and say we gave it the old college try, and then when we leave this McDonald's, we can leave as friends. This is not going to work."

And I meant it. It really wasn't any negotiating ploy. I just couldn't bear looking him in the eye and telling him I only had $750,000 to work with.

So that's where we left it. We left the McDonald's. I called my investors and told them the deal had fallen through.

Later the next day, I talked again with one of the investors. He told me, "Pat, I've made a lot of deals in my life. You can relax about this. It may not be today, maybe not tomorrow, but someday soon, three days, three months, three years, Carl's gonna call you back. You just be patient."

I told him I wished that I felt that way, but I just didn't.

Friday passed. It was a horrible weekend, but I got through it. Monday morning, I went back to work, and about 9:30 in the morning, my secretary came in and told me, "Carl's on the phone for you."

I picked up the phone, said, "Hello." I heard the first words out of Carl's mouth to me since we had parted company at that McDonald's: "You little so-and-so. I didn't sleep good all weekend, and I hope you didn't, either."

I laughed and said, "Well, Carl, I just can't tell you how heartbroken I am that we couldn't get this together."

Then, without any transition at all, he just said, "Tell them six-fifty. That's my bottom line."

I could hardly believe my ears. I said, "Are you serious?"

He said, "Yes, I'm serious. That's all we can go, but we'll take six-fifty."

I said, "Carl, I called all my investors and told them that the deal was off. I guess I'm about to call them all back to make sure they're good to go with this. But assuming they are, Carl, I think you just sold a bank."

I set up a meeting and got all my investors together, and the strangest thing happened. One of them looked me in the eye and said, "Hickman, you gave up too easy."

I said, "What do you mean?"

He said, "Well, if he dropped that much after one conversation, that means he would've dropped more than that if you'd asked him to. You can probably get this deal done for $600,000. You have to try for that."

I just stared at him. He actually wanted me to go back and try to get a lower price...after I had personally agreed to a figure that was less than what my board of directors had said was my maximum!

I said, "You don't understand. I made an agreement with the man."

He didn't care. This one investor kept insisting I had to try to renegotiate the deal. He was loud, he was boisterous, he was insistent. And the rest of the investors agreed with him.

I said, "Guys, guys you're killing me here. Listen: I work for you. If that's what you tell me to do, I'll go back there, and I will try to renegotiate this. But I have to tell you, this is not a good thing you're asking me to do."

They told me to do it anyway. So I said I would.

I left that meeting, I spent a little time working on my courage, I picked up the phone, and I called Carl.

We traded hellos and such, and then I said, "Carl, I want to renegotiate the price."

There was a little pause. He said, "What do you mean?"

"Well," I said, feeling more than a little shaky, "I talked to my investors, and we want to get it for 600."

Carl's tone was suddenly icy. Over the phone, he told me, "Pat, that price just went up to 750. And if you try to negotiate, the deal is off."

I took a deep breath. Then I said, "I don't blame you one bit, sir. We will pay the 750." And I meant it.

We said goodbye. And we hung up.

I went back to my guys, and I said, "Okay. Here's the deal. Here's how the conversation went. He heard what I wanted, he didn't like it, and he told me that the price is now 750. Not only that. He told me that if I were to try to negotiate on the price at all, the whole deal was out the window. I have given the man my word we were going to pay $750,000 for his share in this bank, and by damn, that's what we're going to pay for it. If that costs me your support, so be it. You guys can get out if you want, but if you stay in, I need to say two things. First and foremost, one way or another, I am going to keep my word to Carl. Second, please don't ever ask me to go back on my word like that again. I cannot, I will not do that, ever again."

None of the investors gave me any static. We bought the bank for $750,000. Now, I realize that $100,000 may sound like a lot of money, and that some people might say we lost that $100,000. In fact, that was a very small price to pay for the lesson we all learned from that experience. We don't go back on our word.

Let's get very clear on what happened to Pat here, because it's the same thing that needs to happen to us as we live an authentic life. It's one thing to say we believe something, but when our actions consistently align with our words, that is living proof that we believe it.

Pat taught the true understanding of knowing what you believe. And when you really believe something, it drives and shows up in everything you do. This is not a sometimes thing. It is an all-the-time thing.

Pat's understanding of his values and, ultimately, the bank's values separated him in a market filled with unlimited banking choices. And, we saw firsthand that the very best in the banking industry wanted to work with and for Pat.[2]

When you are truly authentic, you make decisions that align with your values even when they seemingly cost you profits or personal gain. When your actions scream what you really believe, people fully know who you are and what you stand for. Great values and truly authentic people naturally attract others to their mission and their cause. Authenticity is at the core of being a great leader. When people know where you stand, they can depend on you, they trust you, and they want to be around you.

When we don't know what we truly believe, we are easily influenced by the loudest voice in the room. And, the loudest voice isn't necessarily the right voice. Anyone can make the easy decision. How do you respond when the easy decision doesn't fully align with what you say you believe? It's at this moment that everyone knows what you truly believe and where your authenticity lies.

---

2. If you would like to discover more about the amazing story of Happy State Bank and learn from the leadership of J. Pat Hickman, check out the book, *Non-Negotiable*.

TAPPING INTO YOUR AUTHENTICITY

When you can understand and tap into your authenticity, you will not only create possibilities for yourself but also those around you. To discover how to live your authenticity, think about the following:

Individually:

- Identify your core values: what principles are nonnegotiable for you?

- Reflect on moments when you felt most "yourself": what were you doing?

- Pay attention to emotional dissonance: where are you pretending or posturing?

- Stop comparing yourself to others; your path is uniquely yours.

- Speak your truth, even when it's uncomfortable.

- Let go of roles and expectations that don't fit who you are.

As a leader:

- Clarify your leadership philosophy: what do you believe, and how do you show it?

- Align your public persona with your private values.

- Admit mistakes and be honest about your journey.

- Ask, *Where am I performing instead of leading?*

DON'T BUY THIS JACKET

In 2011, Patagonia, known for its quality outdoor gear and deep commitment to sustainability, launched a bold campaign featuring the message: "Don't Buy This Jacket." The ad, showcasing one of their own best-selling products, wasn't a gimmick. It was a genuine call to reduce consumerism and environmental impact. In a world where marketing is designed to boost sales, Patagonia's message stood out as astonishing and deeply authentic.

This campaign wasn't a contradiction; it was a reflection of Patagonia's core values. The company has always prioritized environmental responsibility over profit. They don't just make eco-friendly products, they challenge their customers to consume less and think critically about what they buy. That's what it means to live your authenticity.

Patagonia backs its words with action. They were early adopters of recycled polyester and organic cotton, long before it became an industry trend. They are a certified Fair Trade company, ensuring safe working conditions and fair pay for the people who make their clothes. While other companies may talk about values, Patagonia invests in them, often at higher cost, because it's what they truly believe.

In 2017, the company went even further, suing the US government to protest the reduction of national monuments in Utah. That bold legal action, taken to protect public lands, showed that Patagonia doesn't just meet environmental standards, it fights for them.

In addition to bold campaigns and legal advocacy, Patagonia's long-standing recycling and repair programs further underscore its commitment to sustainability. Through the Worn Wear initiative, customers are encouraged to trade in used gear, buy refurbished items, and repair what they already own. Patagonia even sends out mobile repair trucks across the country to fix zippers, patch jackets, and breathe new life into well-loved gear, often for free.

The company also offers take-back programs for garments at the end of their life, recycling old pieces into new textiles whenever possible. In doing so, Patagonia helps close the loop on apparel waste, one of the fashion industry's biggest environmental challenges.

These efforts are not just add-ons, they are baked into the business model. Patagonia doesn't merely aim to reduce harm, it actively seeks to regenerate and sustain. That's what makes them astonishing; they lead not by selling more, but by asking better of themselves and their customers.

Today, Patagonia is one of the most respected companies in the world, not just because of its products, but because of its unwavering commitment to its values. In an age when many companies treat "values" as marketing copy or wall art, Patagonia lives theirs every day.

That's the real lesson—your actions, not your slogans, reveal what you truly believe. Whether you're building a life or a company,

Your actions, not your slogans, reveal what you truly believe.

authenticity comes from aligning what you do with what you say. Patagonia proves how powerful that alignment can be.

UNDER THE HOOD

There lives a company high up in a mountain town in the western United States. Two young men dreamed of building a lifestyle business in a mountain community. And they did just that. They manufacture hoodies, which are not your average hoodies. This company has great designs, excellent manufacturing techniques, and incredible fabrics. Everything is in place to explode their business.

They have grown over the years and now employ 65 people, all residents of the small mountain community where they live.

Here's where it gets interesting. This company only sells in its single store in that mountain town. You can't buy most products online, no mail order. To enter their store, you need an appointment. Unless you are incredibly fortunate to snag a cancellation, getting an appointment will probably take nine months or longer. Once you manage to secure that appointment and plan your trip to reach the store in this small town way up in the mountains, you're only allowed to purchase two items. That's it. After all that, you might expect them to charge a premium for their incredible hoodies that are so hard to obtain. However, it's exactly the opposite; they sell everything at very reasonable prices.

Now, you're probably wondering, *What's the name of this store?* Well, they do not want to be interviewed because they do not want the additional exposure. They are worried that an increase in demand would put additional strain on their customers and do not want to disappoint people. So, we've decided not to reveal their name.

The owners of this company could sell online. They could move significantly more products and generate much more revenue. However, to do so, they would need to relocate their manufacturing offshore and alter their relationship with their town and neighbors. Simply put, they are not inclined to take that path. What makes them astonishing is not just that they create an excellent product, sell it at a highly competitive price, and provide numerous jobs for their community, but they are also dedicated to upholding their beliefs and the ideals upon which they built their company.

They truly have passion, innovation, and work hard. Driving all that is a commitment to their authentic selves, beliefs, and vision of what their lives and the lives of everyone working with them can be. Their authenticity drives their astonishing organization and impacts the entire community in which they live.

OUTPACING OTHERS' BELIEFS OF WHO YOU ARE

In a world that often views communication challenges and social differences as limitations, some individuals defy expectations and turn those differences into powerful strengths. Temple Grandin is one of those people.

Diagnosed with autism at a young age, Temple struggled with verbal communication, social interaction, and intense sensory sensitivity. She screamed, hummed, and avoided human contact. Experts told her parents she should be institutionalized. But her mother refused to accept that future, choosing instead to fight for Temple's place in society and support her development.

With her mother's persistence and the guidance of key mentors, Temple began to navigate the world in her own way. She discovered a deep connection with animals, especially livestock, and found both her passion and purpose in understanding them. While she faced difficulties with traditional social cues, Temple had an extraordinary gift: she thought in pictures. Her mind worked visually, allowing her to understand systems, space, and animal behavior in ways others couldn't.

Instead of seeing autism as a barrier, Temple used her unique perspective to innovate. Her visual thinking gave her an uncanny ability to empathize with animals, particularly cattle. She didn't just observe them, she could feel their stress and discomfort. Using this insight, she redesigned livestock handling systems to make them more humane and efficient. Her revolutionary work, including her design for the cattle chute, is now used in more than half of all cattle-processing plants in the US.

Temple also invented the "squeeze machine," inspired by the cattle equipment she saw on her aunt's ranch. The device applied gentle pressure to calm her own body during moments of sensory overload. What began as a personal solution became a widely recognized tool for others with autism.

Through her designs, her writing, and her public speaking, Temple Grandin bridged the worlds of agriculture and neurodiversity. She showed that autism isn't a limitation, it's a different way of thinking that, when understood and embraced, can drive powerful innovation.

Temple Grandin is a living example of what it means to live authentically. She didn't try to mold herself to fit societal norms. Instead, she leaned into her strengths, accepted her differences, and turned them into her greatest assets. In doing so, she not only transformed an industry but also changed how the world sees autism.

Temple didn't overcome her challenges by hiding who she was, she succeeded by embracing her true self. And that authenticity is what makes her life truly astonishing.

AS A LEADER, HOW DO YOU HELP OTHERS LIVE THEIR AUTHENTICITY?

As a leader, helping others live their authenticity starts with asking values-based questions such as, "What matters most to you in your work?" These questions invite people to reflect on who they are and how that connects to what they do. Give your team permission to bring their full selves to the table, not just their roles or resumes, but their ideas, passions, and lived experiences.

Reward honesty and vulnerability when people are brave enough to share authentically, and celebrate the unique perspectives, styles, and approaches that emerge as a result. Create opportunities for employees to tell their stories, whether through team meetings, internal spotlights, or informal conversations, reinforcing that who they are matters.

Encourage alignment between personal values and professional responsibilities by helping individuals see how their work supports something meaningful to them. Reject the notion of conformity, instead, expect contribution through uniqueness, recognizing that diverse expression strengthens the organization.

Above all, lead by example. The more authentic you are, the more you create an environment where others feel safe and inspired to do the same. Authenticity spreads when it's seen, felt, and consistently lived.

ADDING UP THE PRINCIPLES

Fueling your fire is essential for living your authenticity because it connects you to what is most real within you. Passion is often the purest signal of who you truly are, what excites you, moves you, and keeps you coming back even when things get hard. When you honor that passion, you stop chasing what's expected and start following what feels true. You begin to make choices that reflect your inner values, rather than external pressures. Fueling your fire means protecting that spark, nurturing it with time, energy, and care, so that your life doesn't just look good from the outside, but feels aligned on the inside. It's not about noise or performance—it's about living in sync with what matters most to you. When you live this way, you radiate a kind of quiet power that is unmistakably authentic.

Freeing your mindset allows you to break free from inherited expectations, rigid norms, and outdated definitions of success. When your mind is constrained by fear, convention, or comparison, you end up living someone else's version of life rather than your own. Freeing your mindset means giving yourself permission to imagine new possibilities, to ask, "What if?" and "Why not?" and to design a life that actually reflects who you are. It's about stepping outside the boxes you've been handed and exploring what truly resonates with your values, your story, and your voice. Creativity isn't just about artistry; it's about courage, the courage to think differently, to question the obvious, and to trust your own instincts. Only when your mindset is free can your authenticity fully come alive.

Outworking your ordinary is where your true self isn't just found, it's forged. Living authentically isn't a passive act; it requires relentless effort to align your daily choices with your deepest values, especially when it's inconvenient, uncomfortable, or unpopular. Outworking your ordinary means refusing to coast or conform. It's the discipline of showing up, again and again, for what matters most to you, even when no one's watching. The journey to authenticity is filled with resistance—from within, from others, and from a world that often prefers polish over truth. But when you commit to doing the hard, honest work of becoming who you really are, without shortcuts or masks, you build a life that's not only real, but deeply rooted. And that kind of life can't be shaken.

Forging your resilience is critical for living your authenticity because staying true to yourself often means standing in the face of resistance, doubt, and unexpected setbacks. Authentic living isn't smooth or simple, it's courageous. It requires you to keep going when things get hard, to hold onto your values when they're tested, and to rise again when you falter. Resilience gives you the strength to navigate the discomfort that can come with breaking norms, setting boundaries, or walking a path that others might not understand. Without resilience, authenticity becomes fragile, easily shaken by criticism, fear, or failure. But with resilience, your truth becomes unbreakable. You learn not only how to endure, but how to evolve without losing who you are. It's what allows your authenticity to be more than a moment; it makes it a way of life.

HOW TO LIVE YOUR AUTHENTICITY

Living your authenticity isn't a one-time event. It's a daily discipline. It's the ongoing commitment to align your choices, your voice, and your impact with who you truly are and what you deeply believe. The stories we've shared, Pat Hickman's unwavering integrity, Patagonia's bold consistency, the mountain-town hoodie company's intentional simplicity, and Temple Grandin's fearless individuality, all highlight one unshakable truth: *Authenticity is built by design, not default.*

The following are five steps to take toward living your authenticity and living an astonishing life:

1. Clarify What You Truly Believe

Before you can live your truth, you have to know what that truth is. What do you value, deeply, consistently, nonnegotiably? If you haven't already, take the time to articulate your core values. These are your internal guideposts.[3]

> Pat Hickman didn't have to "figure it out" in the moment; he knew who he was. That's how he knew what to do.

2. Audit Your Actions

Look at how you're spending your time, where you say "yes," and what you tolerate. Do those things reflect your values or contradict them? Alignment isn't about perfection, it's about course correction. Authentic people constantly evaluate if they're living in integrity.

---

3. Use tools like www.valuesworksheet.com to gain clarity.

Temple Grandin didn't fit a mold, and she never tried to. She evaluated what worked for her and courageously built a life around it.

3. Speak with Your Actions

Words might express your values, but actions confirm them. The world isn't waiting to hear what you believe, it's watching to see what you do when it's inconvenient. Are you making decisions that cost you something in the short term but keep you aligned long term?

When Patagonia said, "Don't Buy This Jacket," they weren't running a campaign. They were keeping a promise.

4. Protect Your Non-Negotiable Core Values

What values do you refuse to compromise, no matter the pressure? Write them down. Share them with people who can help you live them. If you don't protect them, you'll drift from them.

Pat Hickman stood in front of his investors and said, "I will keep my word." That was authenticity in action.

5. Lean Into Your Uniqueness

Your authenticity isn't about fitting in, it's about standing out. When you operate from your true self, you stop trying to be "good at them" and start being great at you. That's when you become astonishing.

The hoodie makers in the mountains chose to stay small, stay real, and stay connected to their town. In doing so, they built something no one else could replicate.

BRINGING IT TOGETHER

Authenticity is your superpower. Not a marketing strategy. Not a brand buzzword. It's the only path to becoming truly astonishing.

And the truth is, most people never get there. Why? Because it's easier to copy than to create. It's safer to pretend than to be vulnerable. But astonishing people and organizations don't settle for safe. They choose real.

Living your authenticity means honoring the things you believe, even when no one else is watching. It means choosing values over convenience, truth over popularity, and purpose over profit. It's not always easy, but it's always worth it.

You don't have to be perfect. You just have to be honest. The world doesn't need another imitation, it needs you. Fully. Boldly. Unapologetically.

So here's the real question: Are you willing to be who you truly are, even when it costs you something, so you can build a life, a business, or a legacy that no one else can duplicate?

Because when you live your authenticity, you stop chasing astonishing—and start becoming it.

Chapter 8

LOVE PEOPLE

We shared earlier how action follows belief. It goes even deeper, however. Your beliefs drive your actions. And you can reverse-engineer what anyone believes simply by observing their actions. People know what you believe because they can see how you act.

When at the end of a long travel day, I'm tired and just want to get into my hotel room, and the person at the front desk is a little "chatty," how do I respond? Because how I do reveals exactly how I see people. Do I take a moment to ask how his day is? Do I just put my head down and disengage? If I believe it's important to respect people, then how I interact with them will make my beliefs immediately apparent. How you treat people not only significantly impacts their lives but also yours.

All of the individuals we observed, spoke with, and researched for this book showed similar traits. They all prioritized others in their actions. They focused on the journeys of others rather than being consumed by their own. They believed that all people are essential. They believed that we all face challenges at some point in our lives. And, they believed that we're in this together. Ultimately, they loved people. Loving people activates the thunder in others.

Loving people activates the thunder in others.

Love is a selfless commitment to the growth, well-being, and flourishing of another person. It's about consistently choosing to care, support, and value someone not for what they give you, but for who they are.

Loving people means:

- *Seeing their value* even when they can't see it themselves.

- *Being present* emotionally, mentally, and spiritually when it matters most.

- Speaking truthfully and kindly, even when it's hard.

- *Wanting the best for them,* even if it doesn't benefit you.

- *Forgiving freely* because you understand we're all in process.

- *Encouraging growth* because real love doesn't enable harm or complacency.

- *Respecting their boundaries,* their story, and their journey.

Love is about devotion, compassion, empathy, grace, integrity, and consistency. It's action. It's showing up again and again with patience, humility, and an open heart. You can love a friend, a family member, a colleague, or even a stranger in this way, by choosing to honor their humanity and actively invest in their good.

When you love people and make it about them, you create a place where people want to be. And because you are always looking for the potential in people and leading them to that potential, they naturally feel better about themselves when they are around you.

No journey is traveled alone. Are you actively looking to help others on their journey? Do you recognize the people helping you on yours? When you help people on their journey, they will naturally want to help you on yours. This creates mutual success.

Are we taking the time (making the time) to get to know people? When you get to know someone, know their story, you understand them at a deeper level, you can serve them at a deeper level, and you will make a deeper connection and impact. What we believe about people dictates how we see and treat them.

When you love people and make it about them, you create a place where people want to be.

What we believe about people dictates how we see and treat them.

LOVE TO HIRE

Born in the US and managing a call center in Mumbai, Leila Janah saw inequality firsthand. She witnessed how poverty and lack of opportunity held back millions with untapped potential. It wasn't that people lacked talent, it was that they lacked access. And that realization changed everything for her.

Leila didn't want to rely on charity or short-term aid. She wanted to create lasting change by giving people the tools to lift themselves out of poverty. It wasn't enough to just help them survive—she wanted to empower them to thrive. Her belief was simple but profound: when you truly *love people*, you invest in their potential.

That belief led her to found Samasource, a social enterprise that connects people in underserved communities with digital work, like data processing and transcription, after providing them with the training they need. Her focus on dignified, fair-paying jobs gave people a way into the global economy, helping them build better futures for themselves and their families.

Samasource has continued to grow as a global leader in socially responsible outsourcing, now known as Sama. Its model has helped lift more than 60,000 people out of poverty, with workers earning wages that often double or triple their previous income. Beyond employment, Sama invests in career advancement, education, and support services, ensuring its impact is holistic and long-term. By turning digital work into a bridge to opportunity, Leila's vision redefined what ethical innovation looks like, showing that business can be a force for justice, not just profit.

Leila's story is a powerful example of what it means to *love people* in action. She believed in people's ability to transform their own lives, she just helped open the door. Even after her passing in 2020, her legacy lives on through the jobs she created and the lives she touched. Leila didn't just talk about love, she built something that proved it.

BAKING IN LOVE

In a world where second chances are rare, Greyston Bakery exists to offer exactly that, an opportunity for people to rebuild their lives with dignity. Rooted in the belief that incarceration should be about rehabilitation, not lifelong punishment, Greyston gives individuals with criminal records a real chance at employment, growth, and reintegration into society.

Founded in 1982 by Bernie Glassman, a Zen Buddhist monk, the bakery began as a way to provide meaningful work for his students in Yonkers, New York, a community struggling economically. But Glassman quickly saw a bigger need. Many people, especially those with criminal histories, were shut out of the job market entirely. So he introduced Open Hiring®, a revolutionary model with no background checks, no interviews, and no resumes. If you're ready to work, you're hired. Instead of leading with judgment, Greyston shows its genuine love of people through its hiring and training process.

This radical act of *loving people through opportunity* doesn't stop at the door. Greyston offers training, support, and development to help employees grow personally and professionally. It's not just about a paycheck, it's about restoring self-worth and creating a path forward.

When you support Greyston, you're not just enjoying a sweet treat, you're becoming part of a mission to give individuals a chance to change their lives. A mission built around loving people.

TAPPING INTO YOUR LOVE OF PEOPLE

When you can understand and tap into your love of people, you will not only create possibilities for yourself but also those around you. To discover how to truly love people, think about the following:

Individually:

- Reflect on how others have impacted your life; gratitude fuels connection.

- Practice empathy; seek to understand before seeking to be understood.

- Be fully present; attention is a powerful form of love.

- Acknowledge your own humanity to better embrace others' imperfections.

- Make kindness a daily discipline, not a random act.

- Notice your assumptions and judgments; loving people starts with seeing them clearly.

As a leader:

- Ask, *Do I see the people or just the performance?*

- Challenge the narrative that love and leadership are incompatible.

- Prioritize relationships over transactions.

- Reflect on who you lead with love, and who you might be unintentionally overlooking.

- Don't treat people differently.

BULLY-FREE ZONE

We often tell ourselves we're not ready to make a difference, that we need more time, experience, or resources. But the truth is, change begins the moment we decide to start. It doesn't take grand gestures; it takes love, kindness, and one small action at a time.

That's exactly what Cavanaugh Bell discovered. After being bullied at age six, he decided he couldn't stand by while others suffered. Too young to volunteer formally, Cavanaugh didn't wait for permission, he created his own nonprofit, Cool & Dope, to fight bullying and empower kids to speak up.

His commitment caught the attention of local leaders. He met with the mayor of Gaithersburg, Maryland, and helped establish Bullying Awareness Day and Bullying Prevention Month in his community. By age eight, he had already made a measurable impact, proving that love and action, not age, are what drive real change.

Cavanaugh had already done more for others than many adults do in a lifetime. His efforts extended far beyond just spreading awareness; he took tangible steps to make a difference in his community and beyond. Everything Cavanaugh had achieved, all the change he had created, had been driven by a single, powerful force—his love for people.

And that's precisely why his story does not stop there.

When the Covid pandemic hit, Cavanaugh's mission grew. Worried about his grandmother in assisted living, he used $640 of his own savings to create a care pack for her. Then he thought, *What about her friends?* That one act of love sparked a wave of generosity. News coverage inspired donations, and soon Cavanaugh had opened the Love is Greater Than COVID-19 Community Pantry in his hometown.

And again, he didn't stop there. With the help of supporters, he sent two 53-foot trucks full of supplies to the Pine Ridge Indian Reservation, one of the poorest communities in the US.

Cavanaugh's story proves that loving people, through action, not just intention, is how movements begin. Each time he recognized a need, his love for people stirred him to act, embracing each new opportunity with purpose and compassion. He didn't wait to be older, richer, or more prepared. He simply cared, and then did something about it. And that's how ordinary moments become extraordinary impact.

MAJOR LOVE

In the late summer of 1977, in the panhandle of Texas, a young woman went off to college at West Texas State. Like many women attending college, one of her primary goals was to join a sorority. When this young lady showed up for sorority rush, she was promptly informed that she could not participate with the other 400 women and was dismissed.

Being a black woman in West Texas had its own meaning in 1977, and in that situation, it meant you could not join a sorority. That young woman, Sharon Miner, left school not long after that incident, but her heart was not hardened. Sharon was not bitter. She worked to create a better world for everyone around her.

In the 1990s, Sharon returned to West Texas State, which had become West Texas A&M University, and graduated. Sharon interned for a US congressman. Then she worked for a state senator who became the ambassador to Sweden. Sharon also had the opportunity to meet with President George W. Bush on several occasions. A few years later, after all of her philanthropic work in the community and for the university, Sharon was honored as a distinguished alumnus of West Texas A&M University.

You might read this brief snippet of a remarkable woman's life and think that she is astonishing, but you don't have the entire story. And, you don't have critical insights into what makes Sharon amazing.

Sharon and her friend, Susan Wegner, founded Princess Ministries more than 20 years ago as a way of serving others. For many years, they held monthly birthday parties for all the children of single mothers staying in a shelter. They threw a fabulous party and ensured the children had plenty of presents. Sharon knows that without these parties, these children would not receive any birthday presents or be celebrated for the amazing young people they are. The impact she had on these children is immeasurable.

Additionally, Sharon makes sure the senior girls at Cal Farley's Boys Ranch have a senior tea party and showers them with lovely gifts. These critical life events can shape a young person's life, and Sharon is there to ensure that no one falls behind.

And, if that all wasn't enough, every week Sharon visits a local home in Amarillo for women who are recovering from challenges with substance abuse. Each week, Sharon brings inspiration, support, and essential biblical teachings for the women there who are fighting to regain control over their lives, self-respect, and a meaningful direction to move forward.

I (SS) have had the honor of working with Sharon for five years, and I have experienced firsthand the tenacity and commitment Sharon has for the ideals she believes in. Sharon believes in the innate goodness of all people. Sharon believes in the expansive potential of all people. And Sharon believes in the critical importance of giving grace to all people as "we all mess up at times."

Yes, Sharon fuels her fire, frees her mindset, outworks her ordinary, forges resilience, and lives authentically. But more than all of those definitive attributes of being an astonishing person, Sharon loves people. It shows in the way she sees, treats, and commits to people. Everyone around Sharon is better for her presence.

AS A LEADER, HOW DO YOU HELP OTHERS LOVE PEOPLE?

As a leader, helping others love people begins by modeling love yourself, through consistent care, fairness, and genuine connection. Show your team that relationships matter by making time for personal conversations and getting to know people beyond their roles. Speak life into your team by offering words of encouragement and affirmation; the right words at the right time can have a lasting impact.

Create meaningful traditions that honor people's contributions and celebrate their stories, reinforcing that everyone matters and belongs. Build trust not just through consistency, but through compassionate truth-telling, being honest in a way that uplifts and respects.

Encourage team members to support and celebrate one another, fostering a culture of appreciation and kindness. Recognize emotional labor, especially from those who consistently uplift others, and make sure they know their efforts are seen and valued.

Above all, remind your team that lasting impact comes through relationships, not just through results. When people love people, they don't just work together, they build something extraordinary together.

ADDING UP THE PRINCIPLES

Fueling your fire is vital to truly loving people because it roots your care in purpose and makes your presence more powerful. When your work and life are driven by authentic passion, you show up with energy, attentiveness, and a genuine desire to contribute, not out of obligation, but out of love. People can feel when you're doing something with your whole heart. Passion sustains compassion; it keeps you engaged even when loving others is hard, inconvenient, or thankless. It helps you stay present, listen deeply, and serve generously. Fueling your fire doesn't just make you more productive, it makes you more human. And when you live from that place, people don't just feel supported, they feel seen, valued, and deeply cared for.

Freeing your mindset breaks down the mental barriers that limit empathy, understanding, and connection. When you release rigid assumptions, biases, and inherited definitions of worth, you begin to see others more clearly and love them more fully. A free mindset allows you to meet people where they are, not where you think they *should* be. It opens you to discover different stories, cultures, needs, and truths without judgment. This openness fosters deeper listening, more inclusive compassion, and a radical kind of love that honors individuality rather than expecting conformity. To truly love people, you have to let go of the boxes you've been taught to put them in, and that begins with freeing your own mind.

Outworking your ordinary is important to love people because true love, especially in action, often requires going beyond what's comfortable or convenient. It means showing up even when you're tired, listening even when it's easier to speak, and giving your best when no one is watching. Loving others deeply isn't always easy or instant—it takes effort, consistency, and a willingness to serve in small, unseen ways. By choosing to outwork your ordinary, you demonstrate a love that's not just emotional but embodied, one that sacrifices, sustains, and supports others through real action. It says, "You matter enough for me to go the extra mile." In doing so, you transform love from a feeling into a force.

Forging your resilience is essential to loving people because real love endures, not just in moments of joy, but especially through difficulty, disappointment, and change. People are complex, and relationships often come with setbacks, misunderstandings, or pain. Without resilience, it's easy to retreat, shut down, or give up when love gets hard. But when you've built inner strength, you can hold space for others even when they're hurting or hurting you. You can stay grounded when circumstances are turbulent. Resilience allows you to keep showing up with compassion and courage, to forgive, to heal, and to keep choosing love even when it costs something. It's what makes love not just tender, but durable.

Living your authenticity contributes to loving people because true connection can only grow from truth. When you show up as your real self, unmasked, unfiltered, and aligned with your values, you give others permission to do the same. Authenticity removes the barriers of performance and pretense, allowing love to be rooted in who you are, not who you're trying to be. It creates safety, trust, and depth in relationships because people know they are encountering someone genuine. More than that, when you live authentically, your love becomes an extension of your wholeness, not an effort to fill a void or earn approval. It's love given freely, not conditionally. And that's the kind of love that transforms lives.

HOW TO LOVE PEOPLE

Loving people isn't about sentiment, it's about seeing their worth and choosing action. The astonishing individuals and organizations in this chapter didn't just care, they showed up, created systems, gave second chances, and sparked hope. They didn't wait to be asked. They didn't make it about themselves.

They loved people, on purpose.

The following are seven steps to take toward loving people and living an astonishing life:

1. See People's Potential, Even When They Don't

Don't just look at where someone is. Look at what's possible for them. Love means holding a vision for others until they can see it for themselves.

Leila Janah saw genius in overlooked communities. Her love translated into opportunity and dignity through meaningful work.

2. Lead with Presence, Not Performance

You don't need perfect words or solutions. You need to show up, with consistency, curiosity, and care. Love is attention.

Sharon Miner throws birthday parties and tea parties not for show, but because people matter. She sees who others often overlook.

3. Choose Action Over Sympathy

Feeling for someone is good. Doing something for them is better. Love lives in action: packing care kits, writing the check, making the call, offering the job.

Cavanaugh Bell didn't wait to be old enough to lead. At six, he started with what he had. That's love in motion.

4. Honor Every Story

We can't love what we don't understand. Listen. Learn someone's story. Don't assume you know. When you know someone's journey, judgment falls away, and compassion takes its place.

> Greyston Bakery skips the résumé. Their open hiring policy starts with trust, not background checks. That's loving people before knowing them.

5. Create Systems That Serve

Love isn't always individual. Sometimes, it's organizational. Build cultures, teams, and policies that reflect how much people matter.

> Leila Janah didn't just help people one by one, she built a global enterprise that gave thousands the chance to rewrite their story.

6. Extend Grace Freely

We all fall short. Real love forgives, believes again, and gives another chance. Grace opens the door for redemption and renewal.

> Sharon Miner meets women in recovery every week with faith, truth, and compassion. Her grace helps them rebuild their lives.

7. Start Now, No Matter Your Age, Title, or Resources

You don't need permission to love. You don't need a nonprofit, a platform, or a big bank account. You just need the courage to start.

> Cavanaugh Bell didn't wait until he was "ready." He acted from love, and the world followed his lead.

BRINGING IT TOGETHER

To be astonishing is to love people fiercely, intentionally, and without conditions.

Love is the force that transforms potential into progress, wounds into wisdom, and lives into legacies. It isn't passive. It's proactive. It moves toward the mess, the need, and the possibility.

Whether you're mentoring someone, hiring differently, celebrating quietly, or standing up for someone who can't, it all counts. Every act of love, however small, echoes beyond the moment.

Leila Janah lifted entire communities. Sharon Miner brought joy to the forgotten. Bernie Glassman gave dignity to those cast aside. Cavanaugh Bell showed us that age doesn't limit impact.

They each proved this truth: Loving people isn't what you do after success—it's how you become truly successful.

When you love people well, they rise. And when people rise, so does the world.

Chapter 9

THE LITTLE THINGS

Sometimes it's the smallest moments, the quietest actions, and the most subtle details that have the greatest impact. We often equate being astonishing with grand gestures that demand attention. However, true greatness is frequently built on little things—the small acts of kindness, the consistency of commitment, and the decisions made day after day, often unseen.

Being astonishing doesn't always require a loud entrance; sometimes, it's about leaving a trail of brilliance in the background, shaping your world with intention, and understanding that the details matter. When you show up fully, even in the smallest ways, you begin to build something that transcends the ordinary, leaving a lasting impression without needing to make a spectacle.

In this chapter, we explore how these seemingly minor actions can accumulate into extraordinary experiences. Whether it's a thoughtful gesture, a moment of genuine care, or an unexpected effort to go above and beyond, these little things have the power to create a profound impact. In a world that celebrates the big moments, it's the subtle, intentional actions that often leave the most lasting impression. The people and organizations that follow embody the core principles we've outlined, showing how the little things truly make the astonishing.

DRIVEN BY EXCELLENCE

All Uber experiences are different. Sometimes the drivers are personable and engaging, and other times not. Some cars are very clean, and

---

Being astonishing doesn't always require a loud entrance; sometimes, it's about leaving a trail of brilliance in the background, shaping your world with intention, and understanding that the details matter.

---

others have trunks half full of stuff that gets in the way of loading your suitcases. Recently, I (SS) had a very unique Uber experience. Dennis picked me up at my home to take me to the airport. He pulled up in his Honda Odyssey, helped load my suitcase into his empty trunk, and I entered a spotless car. I looked around. The car was one of the cleanest cars I've ever been in. I assumed he hadn't had it very long. We chatted, and I commented about his car. Then he surprised me and asked me how many miles I thought the car had. This immediately made me raise the number I would have given initially. I told Dennis I thought he must have 85,000 miles. Dennis chuckled and said, "I have 516,000 miles on this car."

Dennis's passion for his job shines through in every detail, driving him to outwork his ordinary by investing extra care and effort into his vehicle beyond standard upkeep. He freed his mindset by refusing to accept that age and mileage define quality, treating his half-million-mile Odyssey like a brand-new showroom model. For an Uber driver, their automobile is both their office and their product. If an Uber driver wants to give an incredible experience to their clients, they need to make the effort to have an automobile in incredible condition, regardless of age.

A PORTRAIT OF CARE

One of my (SS) favorite pieces of art is titled "Catch of the Day" by world-famous photographer Thomas Mangelsen. This is Mangelsen's signature piece and has been referred to as the "most iconic nature photograph." How I came to own this treasured artist-proof version of his work is a story unto itself, but many years after the picture had hung in my home, my son Geoff commented that he thought it was faded. I looked at it closely and agreed that the piece didn't seem to sparkle like it used to. The colors just didn't have that rich depth anymore.

I wrote to the studio's home office to share our observations and asked what we could do. The woman asked me to send her pictures of the piece. Once they reviewed the pictures, my contact said that they wanted to see the framed picture up close and would send me a wooden crate to return it to them. The picture measures 59 x 39. This is not a small item. After they inspected the photo, they said they would replace it and even offered to frame it in the new, more modern framing style they were offering. The entire experience was totally at their expense.

I never expected this level of care and service when I first contacted the artist's studio. At no time did they try to deflect responsibility. Actually, the studio took full responsibility for the quality of the piece and the costs associated with having it sent back to them for inspection and the eventual replacement.

Here is an organization that wanted its products to be of the highest quality and remain at that level. They never wanted anyone to see one of their pieces in less than pristine condition. Remember, the artist's name is signed on each piece, so his reputation is always on the line.

Ultimately, they want each customer to be thrilled the day they purchase one of Thomas's works of art and to remain that way. This is an astonishing organization in the way they approach each item they sell and each client they serve. Their actions reflect more than just customer service, they reflect a deep passion for their craft, a commitment to excellence, and a profound respect for the people who support their work. By standing behind their art with integrity and going far beyond what was expected, they outworked their ordinary, fueled their fire for quality and legacy, and showed what it truly means to love people through the work they do.

THE POWER OF DETAILS

Each year at their national convention, the National Speakers Association awards the Certified Speaking Professional (CSP) designation to deserving professional speakers who have earned it. This accomplishment takes years to achieve, and it is the highest-earned designation in the speaking industry.

The ceremony takes place on the main stage and in front of all of the members. As they call each recipient's name, the person walks onto the stage, has the medal placed around their shoulders, shakes the hand of the association chairman, and gets acknowledged by the entire audience.

I (SS) personally have had the honor of receiving the medal, placing that medal around the recipients' shoulders, and shaking those hands, so I know just how thrilled everyone is.

One time I was observing from the audience, and I noticed the detail that the woman placing the medal took each time she put a medal around someone's neck. She made sure it was turned the right way, it was straight, and not covered by the person's hair if they had long hair. If the person's collar was messed up, she would straighten it. She was meticulous about how each individual looked as they walked forward to shake the chairperson's hand, have their picture taken, and be applauded by the audience.

I was transfixed by the detail she took to make sure that each person looked fantastic. It was all in the details. This was only a moment in time, but I fully imagine that this person makes an astonishing effort in everything she does. It's an attention to detail—it is not accepting anything less than the best that can be done in a situation.

Many times, "our best" is limited by how we think the job should be done. When we free our minds to what "best" can really be by observing someone go into so much detail, it impacts how we see any job or responsibility. We can be astonishing at even the most mundane of tasks.

CREATING EXCELLENCE THROUGH DETAILS

Don't underestimate the power of the little things. In 2005, High Point University (HPU) had a little over 1,600 students and its campus size totaled 92 acres. Today, the student body exceeds 6,300 and the campus is 560 acres. What happened? Dr. Nido Qubein became the president of the university.

HPU positions itself as The Premier Life Skills University. If you walk around its campus, you see countless water features, spotless grounds, and streets with names like Inspiration Way and Extraordinary Way. You subtly hear classical music being played. And whether you realize it or not, the students are constantly learning how to navigate life's challenges.

It's not enough to have a degree. With the life skills that graduates leave with, HPU graduates not only have a rewarding college experience and a valuable degree, but they are also uniquely prepared to take on the challenges awaiting them in a competitive environment and become valued team members for the companies that hire them.

From the on-campus steak house, Prime 1924, where students are taught how to be interviewed while eating a meal, to the simulated airplane cabin where students learn how to network on a flight, life's lessons are always in play.

And, HPU masters the little things. Arriving on campus for a tour, guests are directed to a parking lot where their name is on a large sign in front of their reserved parking spot. Someone is waiting to escort them in a purple golf cart to the admissions office and for a campus tour. When sitting down to have lunch with Dr. Qubein, a prepared lunch menu with the guest's name is on the place setting. Nothing is left to chance. Every little detail is thought of and addressed. This is intentional leadership, and it is the sign of astonishing leaders.

This attention to detail is what the HPU culture is all about. It is what creates memorable experiences and attracts students and hiring organizations to the campus. Universities compete fiercely for the top candidates. Students have the ability to get a good education at so many schools. If you want to be different, if you want to stand out, and if you want to compete with an absolute competitive advantage in your industry, you need to lead intentionally and create that uniqueness. This way of thinking, with a free mindset, and doing, having outworked their ordinary, is what has led to the fantastic growth and success HPU has enjoyed.

THE DRESS THAT MADE THE NIGHT

Years ago, we attended a family friend's wedding. Christine, the bride, realized during the ceremony that her dress was too tight, making it hard to breathe. As stores were closing, a friend's mom called Nordstrom with just 10 minutes to spare. She explained the situation and asked about available white dresses. The associate replied, "What size? I'll pull what we have, and they'll be ready when you arrive. We'll stay open." After bringing the dresses to the reception, one dress fit perfectly, and Christine danced comfortably all night.

This may have seemed like a small act, but to Christine, it meant everything. By staying open late and preparing options in advance, their associates didn't just offer service, they demonstrated their love of people, offering empathy, urgency, and care that turned a stressful moment into a joyful one. Nordstrom often comes up as a case study for their great service. Their consistent willingness to go above and beyond, even in unexpected situations, shows what it means to treat people with heart and to outwork your ordinary.

MORE THAN A PATIENT

I (AS) met Austin the first day of my first clinical rotation of medical school. Cancer in his bones was ravaging his body one organ system at a time. During our very first encounter, he thanked me for the care I was providing him. I remember being confused as I hadn't yet provided any care. Austin always had his hospital room door open, inviting others into his space. Over the coming weeks, I grew close to him, learning about his life outside of the hospital. He worked in the music industry and once said, "How cool is it that I have found my life's passion in music?"

He was planning a birthday party to bring friends and colleagues together, not just to celebrate, but to help them connect and dream bigger. Austin died before that day came. However, his legacy lives on in those he inspired to pursue their work with passion and purpose. He showed the quiet power of a kind word and intentional presence. Austin was astonishing in how he made others feel seen, welcomed, and valued. Austin created a ripple effect; his presence inspired others to dream bigger, live more intentionally, and lead with kindness simply because they knew him.

Austin embodied the principles of fueling your fire, loving people, and living your authenticity with quiet, powerful grace. Even in the face of terminal illness, he remained rooted in gratitude, passion, and connection, welcoming others into his life with an open door and an open heart. His deep love for music and his desire to bring people together reveal a man who lived fully, purposefully, and generously, making those around him feel not just cared for, but inspired to live more boldly themselves.

A LESSON IN POSSIBILITY

Tim Cerutti was a middle school teacher who transcended expectations and left an indelible mark on the students in his care, impacting confidence, drive, and sense of possibility. Teachers can be astonishing when they see potential in students before the students see it in themselves. They create spaces where curiosity thrives and every question feels worth asking. Through quiet dedication and relentless belief, they change the trajectory of lives, often without even realizing it. Mr. Cerutti accomplished that for many students, and his influence continues to echo in the work they do and the way they strive to lift others. He embodied *the little things* through his everyday attentiveness, encouragement, and the way he made each student feel seen, capable, and worth investing in.

He didn't just teach; he believed. His belief in students' potential helped unlock theirs, creating an environment where growth felt possible and confidence took root, freeing their mindset. By investing in the small, consistent gestures of encouragement and care, Mr. Cerutti quietly outworked the ordinary and left a legacy far beyond the classroom. And, his students went on to explore, achieve, and impact their world in more significant ways because of his actions.

BRINGING IT TOGETHER

In this chapter, we explored how the smallest moments and actions often leave the most lasting and profound impacts. Interwoven among these stories lies each of the principles we have already highlighted: fueling your fire; freeing your mindset; outworking your ordinary; forging your resilience; living your authenticity; and loving people collectively drive each of these astonishing people and organizations.

Whether it's a simple gesture of kindness, attention to detail, or the quiet consistency of showing up, the little things shape our experiences and our connections with others. These seemingly minor acts often become the foundation for extraordinary outcomes, creating the ripple effect we next dive into, one that resonates far beyond the moment. From the dedicated teacher who believed in a student's potential to the Uber driver who maintained his car with remarkable care, these examples remind us that greatness doesn't always have to be grand, it can be built in the everyday moments that go unnoticed by most but are deeply felt by those who experience them.

Through the stories of HPU's attention to detail, the unrestrained customer service at Nordstrom, and the quiet impact of Austin's presence in a hospital room, we see that the power of the little things drives true excellence. These small acts, when done consistently and with intention, create meaningful and unforgettable experiences. Whether in business, personal interactions, or even life-changing moments in a hospital room, the little things, those acts of thoughtfulness, care, and dedication, are what truly set us apart and make us astonishing. In a world that often celebrates the loud and the big, it's the subtle, intentional actions that truly change lives and create lasting impressions.

Chapter 10

THE RIPPLE EFFECT

KELLY SWANSON'S RIPPLE

I (SS) had dinner with a friend of mine who is also a professional speaker. Kelly Swanson is a fantastic storyteller and knows how to touch the hearts of those in her audience. Many other professionals had given Kelly advice on how she should change her market, change her stories, and change her message. They gave this advice, believing it would help her grow her business.

None of this felt true to Kelly. Kelly asked my opinion about whether she should stay with her passion for telling stories that made people laugh, connected to their hearts, and also delivered the important message that Kelly was all about.

Before I could answer her, Kelly shared a story with me about a recent audience member who approached her after a program and said with tears in her eyes, "I was planning my exit strategy, and after I heard your words, it made me realize that I must still be here for a purpose and to keep going."

I simply replied, "Kelly, there's your answer."

What is the value of one life? Your truth will profoundly impact others. Being transparent, true to yourself, and real to those around you sets the stage for being astonishing. Kelly saved the life of a woman that day. How will that woman go on to impact the lives of her children or people in her community? How will the experience that woman had in Kelly's audience affect the way the woman interacts and guides others she comes in contact with? Will that woman go on to be a Nobel Laureate? No one knows, but we do know that she has the opportunity to impact others' lives just because she is here. Kelly's ripple created that opportunity.

You may not realize it, but you're astonishing, or can be. Your actions, your words, and the choices you make every day have the power to change lives, perhaps even the world. Astonishing individuals don't exist in a vacuum, their impact is amplified through the people and environments they influence. This impact can stay with another person for longer than just the short term. Professional

Truly astonishing people spark change beyond themselves.

success is admirable, but if the results begin and end with one person, the ripple effect is limited.

Truly astonishing people spark change beyond themselves. They elevate teams, inspire movements, and leave lasting imprints on the culture around them. Their greatness multiplies, not because they seek recognition, but because their actions awaken possibility in others. You can build a highly successful company and impact the people you work with in profound ways.

SHARON MINER'S RIPPLE

Sharon Miner has had numerous ripples for the young people and adults she has impacted. One such young lady came into her life four years ago while Sharon was working at Martha's Home, a homeless shelter. This lady, Beth, lived in a tent behind a Lowe's store in Amarillo, Texas. Beth had already lost custody of her first child.

Beth shared her experiences of being homeless with Sharon. She also shared that she was pregnant. Sharon immediately worked to get Beth into a program called Present Needs–Future Success, focused on helping women return to school, work toward a livable wage, and get off the streets.

Recently, Beth graduated from Amarillo College, a two-year college, with a 4.0. She is in three individual honor societies and was just accepted to the University of Texas at Arlington. When Beth was inducted into the third honor society, she told Sharon that Sharon was the one who made it happen. Sharon said, "You did the work. You earned the 4.0."

Then Beth said, "But you told me I could."

Beth has a job now as a grant writer for the city of Amarillo. She is about to get her first child back. The grants she writes will change the lives of many people. She will undoubtedly change the lives of her children and many other people she interacts with.

Sharon's ripple is the ability to see the potential in people and then inspire and guide them to reach that potential. Those people go on to impact the lives of others and extend Sharon's ripple.

How do we measure the impact of moments? We can't. No scale can measure the profound shift that occurs when someone's life is touched in a meaningful way. Whether you help one person or one hundred, the depth of your intention will always outweigh the sheer quantity of outcomes.

No scale can measure the profound shift that occurs when someone's life is touched in a meaningful way.

The most astonishing acts come not from seeking recognition or reward, but from a genuine desire to make a difference. It's purity of intention that fuels the ripple effect, propelling it outward in ways we may never fully understand.

Living astonishingly doesn't just happen in isolation. It's a practice, a mindset, and it's contagious. It's important to surround yourself with others who embody the same spirit. Seek out the people who live with humility, courage, generosity, and creativity. These individuals are the models for what greatness looks like in everyday life. They show you that it's possible to live with authenticity and to make a difference in even the most ordinary of circumstances.

THOMAS EDISON'S RIPPLE

One young boy growing up in Michigan in the early 1900s idolized Thomas Edison. His name was Henry Ford. As a teenager, Ford read everything he could about Edison's inventions and was captivated by the way Edison brought ideas to life through relentless trial and error. When Ford finally met Edison at a dinner decades later, he nervously explained his early work on a gasoline-powered engine. Edison's response was simple but powerful: "Young man, that's the thing! You have it! Keep at it!"

That moment lit a fire in Ford. Encouraged by the very inventor he admired most, Ford went on to revolutionize transportation and manufacturing with the Model T and the assembly line. Edison's belief in Ford, just a few words at the right time, helped fuel a movement that would change the world.

The astonishing people around you serve as mirrors, reflecting new possibilities for yourself and others. The more you recognize the brilliance in them, the more your own light shines.

Astonishment is not a finite resource. When you see greatness in others, it doesn't diminish yours, it amplifies it. Together, we create ripples that turn into waves. The power of one person, supported by others on the same path, can change everything.

When you choose to live astonishingly, you become more than just a witness to life, you are an active participant, and you become a catalyst for growth, connection, and transformation. You become a beacon of possibility, a living example of what can happen when you live with intention and purpose. By doing so, you show others that greatness is not something reserved for a select few. Greatness is attainable for all of us. And once you begin to live this way, you'll find that it becomes contagious.

When you see greatness in others, it doesn't diminish yours, it amplifies it.

PAT HICKMAN'S RIPPLE

Pat Hickman has created so many ripples in his life, impacting individuals and organizations in profound ways, that his ripples may be seen as a full-on tidal wave. Many spouses told us that their husbands were better husbands and fathers for having worked with Pat. Think of the impact these men are having on their children and their communities.

One story that was shared with us about Pat was about a young man who, near the end of his senior year in high school, made a

When you choose to live astonishingly, you become more than just a witness to life, you become are an active participant, and you become a catalyst for growth, connection, and transformation.

foolish teenage mistake. This decision could cost him the ability to walk for graduation, be the valedictorian, and possibly cost him his college football scholarship. Pat knew what a fine young man he really was and, unbeknown to the young man, Pat spoke on his behalf. Ultimately, the young man graduated and moved on with his life.

After an illustrious college football career, the young man went on to play in the National Football League (NFL). He cofounded a company and serves as its co-chief executive officer. He was appointed to the Board of Regents of the Texas Tech University System and was named its chairman. This man has impacted the lives of hundreds, if

---

Your life, your legacy, will no longer be measured by the goals you achieve alone. It will be measured by the lives you touch, the hearts you inspire, and the transformations you spark in the people around you.

---

not thousands, of people. His life path would have certainly been different if Pat had not worked to make sure one single bad choice didn't derail what was in place and ready to happen.

Your life, your legacy, will no longer be measured by the goals you achieve alone. It will be measured by the lives you touch, the hearts you inspire, and the transformations you spark in the people around you. Because when you live astonishingly, your impact spreads far beyond your own experience, it creates a ripple effect that is remembered. It leaves a legacy of growth, possibility, and hope.

As you continue on this journey, remember: the ripples you create don't stop with you. They reach far beyond the boundaries of your life. The astonishing path is one that carries forward, building momentum, touching hearts, and leaving a legacy that stretches through time. Each moment you choose to act with intention, each time you dare to be extraordinary, you contribute to a wave of change that will resonate through the lives of countless others.

MICHAEL JORDAN'S RIPPLE

As a kid growing up in Akron, Ohio, LeBron James idolized Michael Jordan. He watched grainy VHS tapes of Jordan's games, memorizing his moves and mimicking his mindset. Jordan wasn't just a basketball player to LeBron, he was proof that greatness was possible through relentless work, unshakable belief, and total commitment.

Years later, LeBron would not only follow in Jordan's footsteps on the court but also build on his legacy off of it. Inspired by Jordan's standard of excellence, LeBron used his platform to create real impact, most notably through the *I PROMISE School*, a public school he founded for at-risk children in his hometown. Michael Jordan taught him how to win. LeBron James turned that inspiration into something even bigger: a mission to lift others and change lives through education, opportunity, and hope.

Each moment you choose to act with intention, each time you dare to be extraordinary, you contribute to a wave of change that will resonate through the lives of countless others.

Astonishing leaders don't just attract talent, they awaken it.

This is the ripple effect—astonishing people are drawn to places that reflect their values and ambitions. They want to contribute to something meaningful. In turn, astonishing organizations are built and sustained by astonishing people, and those organizations, in turn, become magnets for more astonishing people. The cycle begins with leadership. Astonishing leaders don't just attract talent, they awaken it. They help others see who they can become, and in doing so, they cultivate communities where extraordinary becomes the norm.

Chapter 11

BRING THUNDER TO YOUR WORLD

Throughout this book, we explored what it means to be astonishing—not as a performance, but as a way of living, not just once, but consistently as a lifelong habit. We talked about fueling your fire, freeing your mindset, outworking your ordinary, and more.

You don't need to chase greatness, you need to commit to what's true. When you do, the astonishing finds you.

But what does it look like when all of those ideas come together, not in theory, but in the soil of a real life, a real place? This final chapter is about one woman who didn't set out to be extraordinary, yet became a living embodiment of everything this book teaches. Through her hands, her heart, and her vision, a forgotten castle became a sanctuary. Her story reminds us that you don't need to chase greatness, you need to commit to what's true. When you do, the astonishing finds you.

THE CASTLE AND THE COMPASS

Castel Campo is not your typical beacon of transformation. Tucked into the quiet valleys of northern Italy, its stone towers rise like the pages of a fairy tale long forgotten. The walls are ancient. The forest is thick. And, for a long time, it was mostly a relic of the past.

But in walked Marina Clerici, a woman with fierce intuition and quiet strength. Where others could have seen decay, Marina saw invitation. Where others could have seen impracticality, she saw possibility.

She wasn't looking to renovate a castle. She was looking to reclaim a way of living.

Today, Castel Campo serves as a beacon, transformed into a sanctuary of healing, sustainability, and community. With her daughters, Marina founded Campo Base, a nonprofit organization that hosts free summer camps for children and young adults facing chronic illnesses, offering experiences such as trekking, sailing, and wilderness survival skills that empower and uplift them.

The castle grounds also house an organic farm and serve as a hub for cultural and educational events, reflecting Marina's commitment to sustainable tourism and social innovation. Castel Campo is not just a place, it's a living testament to how one woman's passion can ignite lasting change.

Fuel Your Fire

Passion, when it's real, doesn't need to be shouted, it radiates through presence, through effort, through love made visible. Marina didn't need a podium; her fire was in the soil under her nails, the meals shared under open skies, the joy in her tired eyes after another full day of meaningful work. Fueling your fire means finding the place where passion meets purpose, and at Castel Campo, Marina lives that fusion with every step. Her life is proof that when your work flows from what you love, it doesn't burn you out, it burns bright enough to light the way for others.

Castel Campo's passion shines in every detail of its being, from warm welcomes and hand-tended gardens to free summer camps for chronically ill youth and farm-to-table meals that honor the land. Their organic farming and low-impact restoration showcase a deep environmental respect, while cultural residencies and artisan workshops bring fresh creativity to ancient walls. Castel Campo becomes a testament to what's possible when work is driven by passion.

Free Your Mindset

Marina was no stranger to limits. She had been told what was sensible, what was profitable, and what was safe. But she had a habit of asking, *"What if we did it differently?"* What Marina offered wasn't just space, it was permission.

Permission to think differently.

To rest deeply.

To ask bigger questions.

To stop pretending.

In a world obsessed with productivity, she built a place rooted in presence. She asked not, "What are you producing?" but "What are you becoming?" Castel Campo became a living invitation to free your mindset, to return to the quiet truths you've always known but were taught to doubt.

She didn't try to change the world. She changed the frame. And that changed everything. Instead of turning Castel Campo into another commercial venue, she reimagined it as a living ecosystem for people seeking meaning.

Castel Campo frees its mindset by rejecting the idea that a centuries-old castle must remain a museum piece and instead reimagining it as a dynamic, living ecosystem. By asking "What if?" at every turn, Castel Campo continually invents new ways to blend history, sustainability, and community, turning tradition into a springboard for innovation.

Outwork Your Ordinary

There was nothing glamorous about the early days. The buildings needed repairs, and the land was overgrown. But Marina didn't flinch. She showed up. Day after day. Shoveling earth. Restoring stone. Inviting one soul at a time. There were no shortcuts, no big breaks.

She didn't chase "big success." She nurtured small, consistent impact.

And that's how Castel Campo began to wake up, not with a bang, but with a breath.

Marina welcomed people not to a retreat, but to a reconnection. It started with musicians coming to share their craft. Later, it grew to host chefs, actors, and those looking for refuge. The castle became a compass, for those who had lost their way or simply needed to remember who they were.

With its free mindset, the castle became a testament to the principle that relentless mental and physical labor, day after day, brick by brick, idea by idea, transforms vision into reality.

Forge Your Resilience

And resilience? That wasn't some heroic act. It was in the way she kept going. Kept believing. Kept loving the work even when it was heavy.

Marina's resilience wasn't loud or dramatic, it was quiet, steady, and fiercely rooted in purpose. At Castel Campo, when roofs leaked or winters bit hard, she didn't complain, she tended, repaired, and stayed. During the stillness of the pandemic, when guests disappeared and the future felt uncertain, Marina opened her heart wider. She cared for the land, connected with the community, and held space for hope. Her strength wasn't about pushing through; it was about staying true, devoted to the work, the people, and the place. In showing up with quiet determination, she made resilience something others could borrow, feel, and live.

Castel Campo embodies resilience by holding fast to its core mission even as its strategies adapt to meet emerging needs. When circumstances change, the team pivots their programs, refines their offerings, and finds new ways to support and uplift the community without losing sight of their original vision.

Live Your Authenticity

Marina had been many things, a traveler, a student, a seeker, but above all, she was someone who refused to pretend. She didn't contort herself to fit expectations or chase what the world called success. She chose instead to live rooted in truth, her truth. Castel Campo was not a project she took on; it was the embodiment of her values, a living expression of her soul.

Authenticity, as Marina lived it, wasn't a style or a slogan. It wasn't marketing. It was a discipline, a daily, deliberate act of showing up without artifice. To live authentically, she taught us, is to stay in rhythm with what matters: the land, the people, and the deeper purpose that calls us forward. When you live that way, you don't just shift your own life. You transform the lives around you. You make spaces sacred. You make the truth visible. And in doing so, you become astonishing.

Castel Campo lives authentically by aligning every decision, big and small, with values of hospitality, sustainability, and community. Every event, from youth summer camps to artisan workshops, grows organically from the land and people around them, ensuring the castle remains a true expression of its vision rather than a manufactured brand.

Love People

Marina shows she loves people through the way she has poured her heart into Castel Campo, not just as a home, but as a living expression of welcome, belonging, and care. She sees each guest not as a visitor, but as someone worthy of time, presence, and deep listening. Whether she's preparing a meal, sharing the stories of her family's heritage, or simply sitting beside someone in silence, Marina creates space for others to feel seen and heard.

At Castel Campo, love is felt in the details: the thoughtful conversations; the beauty of nature tended with care; the sense that you are not just passing through, but part of something meaningful. Marina's presence at the castle is quiet yet unmistakably powerful, a daily choice to live generously, to open her life to others, and to turn a historic place into a sanctuary of connection and transformation.

At its core, Castel Campo shows its love of people through personalized, heartfelt gestures, greeting each guest by name, sharing communal meals, and tailoring activities to individual needs. Like the family home that records children's growth on a door frame, the castle marks guests' heights by the kitchen, celebrating the extended family and community that bring it to life.

A Living Legacy

Today, Castel Campo stands not as a monument to the past, but as a model for the future. It is astonishing not because it's perfect, but because it's honest. Not because it's profitable, but because it's purposeful.

Marina and Castel Campo teach us that being astonishing creates space for others to do the same. It reminds us that our deepest work is not to impress the world, but to ignite the world by becoming our best selves and being true to who we are.

Castel Campo became more than a destination. It became a movement, a living reminder that when a person lives true to who they are, they awaken a place. A place within them where magic happens and thunder is released with veracity. And when a place is awakened, it calls others to do the same.

So here's the invitation: Don't just visit places like Castel Campo. Become one.

THE ASTONISHING LIFE

Marina's journey is proof that living with intention, heart, and courage can turn even the quietest life into a legacy, because being astonishing isn't about spectacle, it's about impact. However, to be astonishing is not merely to accomplish things, it is to transcend expectations, to illuminate what's possible, and to leave an unmistakable impression of excellence, generosity, and boldness on the world around you.

Being astonishing isn't about spectacle, it's about impact.

At its core, being astonishing begins with vision, a clear goal, yes, but also the courage to move forward even when the path isn't fully visible. Sometimes your vision will feel cloudy. That's not failure, it's process. Clarity comes through action, reflection, and time. Keep moving.

Sometimes your vision will feel cloudy. That's not failure, it's process.

So what does it look like to be astonishing? It looks like someone who shows up fully, who takes risks not just for personal gain but to better their communities, their teams, or even just one other person. It feels like alignment: when your actions, your values, and your voice are in harmony. It feels courageous. It feels like growth. It's unrealistic to embody every astonishing trait at once, all the time, but it's not enough to cling to just one; growth demands that we stretch beyond our strengths and strive for wholeness.

To become astonishing, you cultivate character. You commit to a standard, even when no one's watching. You stay curious, humble, and generous. You become a force that uplifts others, not just by what you do, but by how you do it. To be astonishing is to inspire.

To be astonishing is to inspire.

Astonishing people don't wait for permission. They leverage their superpowers, gifts often rooted in humility and service, and they achieve at levels that exceed what they may have imagined. Pat Hickman didn't set out to become a symbol of extraordinary leadership, he just wanted to run a small bank in Canyon, Texas. And yet, he built something far greater. That's the essence: what begins as ordinary can ripple into the extraordinary when you commit to living with depth, courage, and care.

Astonishing people don't wait for permission.

Why would you want to be astonishing? Because the world is hungry for light, for innovation, for kindness paired with audacity. Because the alternative, being forgettable, or worse, withholding your gifts, leaves too much beauty and power unused.

But here's the truth—being astonishing is not a fixed identity. It's not something you are or aren't. It's something you cultivate. You can be astonishing in one area of life, how you mentor, how you create, how you show up for others, and still be growing in other areas. Astonishing people aren't perfect. They're intentional.

It is not just about having an idea and following through. They aim to make an impact, not necessarily by the numbers, but by the meaning. Helping one person might not make headlines, but it can echo more deeply than helping hundreds. As the proverb reminds us, "If you save one life, it's as if you've saved the whole world."

Astonishing people aren't perfect. They're intentional.

And yes, you can lose it, or feel like you have. No one is astonishing all the time. There will be days when you're tired, off-track, unseen. But the truth is, if you've ever truly been astonishing, it never fully leaves you. It lives in how you've shaped others, and how you keep showing up, even quietly.

Impact is never just about scale. It's about resonance. It's about the lives you touch, the doors you open for others, and the example you set. And yes, intention matters. But so does outcome. What you meant is important, but what you *caused* is what changes the world. Being astonishing is not a destination you arrive at, it's a way of walking through the world. You may have moments when you drift or doubt, but once you've tasted that mindset, the one that demands excellence, that elevates others, that refuses to settle, you'll always feel the pull to return.

Impact is never just about scale. It's about resonance.

Can anyone decide if they're astonishing? Not exactly. Astonishing is something others see in you, often before you see it in yourself. That's the paradox. You control the inputs, your character, your craft, your choices, but "astonishing" is a reflection cast by those impacted by you. And their judgment is rarely about perfection—it's about presence, alignment, and courage.

People recognize astonishing in different ways. And people will recognize different aspects of your astonishing nature. You won't be astonishing to everyone, but you don't need to be. You need to be authentic and intentional. The rest follows.

And here's the final truth: you can never be your very best unless you are helping someone else be their best. Being astonishing isn't about self-recognition, it's about the impact we create for others; it's their growth, healing, or inspiration that gives our actions meaning. The most astonishing people lift others. They inspire growth, not just achievement. They share their light.

And when you surround yourself with astonishing people, something remarkable happens, you start to model each other, sharpen each other, and raise the collective ceiling of what's possible.

You can never be your very best unless you are helping someone else be their best.

You are where you're supposed to be. Now, where are you going? What are you proud of? Where have you lifted others? And what does astonishing look like for you, not in theory, but in practice?

Because the world doesn't need more perfect people. It needs people who dare, who care, who grow, and who give. You already carry the seeds. Surround yourself with others who do too. Recognize the astonishing in them, and it will reflect back to you.

Go bring thunder to your world.

Astonish us.

NOW IT'S YOUR TURN

BE ASTONISHING

You've read the stories. You've explored the principles. Now it's time to live them.

Being astonishing isn't a one-time act; it's a way of showing up, every day, with purpose, conviction, and heart.

IMPLEMENTATION GUIDE

We have a complete 8-week implementation guide for you. And, it's free!

For your free *Be Astonishing...Creating Thunder Implementation Guide* visit: BeAstonishing.com.

SHARE YOUR ASTONISHING
PEOPLE & ORGANIZATIONS

Who in your life or experiences is astonishing? We want to hear about them, your experience, and their impact on you. Share their story at BeAstonishing.com.

ABOUT THE AUTHORS

SAM SILVERSTEIN &
DR. ALLISON SILVERSTEIN

SAM SILVERSTEIN is an internationally recognized authority on accountability, leadership, and workplace culture. As the founder of The Accountability Institute™ and creator of the Certified Accountability Advisor® program, Sam has dedicated his career to helping organizations and individuals build cultures where people thrive and leaders inspire. He is the author of 14 books, including *No More Excuses, The Accountability Advantage, Pivot!,* and *Momentum.*

Recognized as one of the world's top organizational culture professionals, Sam's impact spans boardrooms, classrooms, and communities. Through his powerful keynotes, transformative consulting, and Accountability Roundtables™, he guides leaders to break through the barriers that limit performance and impact and to activate accountability as a strategic advantage.

A former president of the National Speakers Association, Sam has been inducted into the CPAE Speakers Hall of Fame and recognized as a Legend of Professional Speaking. Originally from Atlanta, Georgia, he holds a business degree from the University of Georgia and an MBA from Washington University in St. Louis. Sam lives in St. Louis with his wife and is a proud father of four.

Driven by a deep belief in people's potential to lead with integrity and live with purpose, Sam shows up each day to influence, impact, and transform—and help others do the same.

DR. ALLISON SILVERSTEIN is a Pediatric Palliative Medicine Physician at the University of Colorado and Children's Hospital Colorado, where she serves as the Inpatient Medical Director and Physician Informaticist for the Section of Palliative Medicine. A graduate of esteemed training programs at Texas Children's Hospital in Houston and St. Jude Children's Research Hospital/Le Bonheur Children's Hospital in Memphis, she brings a powerful combination of clinical excellence, academic depth, and compassionate leadership to her work.

Currently serving as Chair of the Pediatrics Council for the American Academy of Hospice and Palliative Medicine, Dr. Silverstein is recognized as a national leader in pediatric care. Her commitment to global health led her to spend two years serving in sub-Saharan Africa, and she further expanded her impact through earning an Executive MBA in Health Administration from the University of Colorado.

Whether caring for children and families at the most vulnerable moments or leading systemic improvements in healthcare, Allison's work is grounded in empathy, presence, and purpose—core traits that align deeply with the message of *Be Astonishing*. Her medical experience has taught her how to listen deeply, act intentionally, and show up fully for others—qualities that inspire those around her to do the same.

Outside the hospital, Allison finds joy in the outdoors—whether running, hiking, or skiing—and treasures the moments that bring balance and reflection.

ACKNOWLEDGMENTS

This book was made possible by the insight, effort, and generosity of many people along the way. Any meaningful achievement is the result of a team, and we are deeply grateful to ours.

We extend our heartfelt thanks to our publisher, John Martin, and the entire team at Sound Wisdom. Your steadfast support, expertise, and dedication have been invaluable, and working with you has been an ongoing joy.

Our sincere appreciation goes to Arjun Rajan for his research and substantial contributions to the book content.

Finally, we wish to thank all those who openly and vulnerably shared their personal stories. Your willingness to offer such honesty added richness, humanity, and depth to these pages, shaping a narrative that is far more meaningful because of you.

Thank you.

BOOK SAM SILVERSTEIN TO SPEAK AT YOUR NEXT EVENT

Contact Us

Sam Silverstein Enterprises, Inc.
The Accountability Institute, LLC
info@SamSilverstein.com
(314) 878-9252

To Order More Copies of
BE ASTONISHING

www.samsilverstein.com

Follow Sam

www.twitter.com/samsilverstein

www.youtube.com/samsilverstein

www.linkedin.com/in/samsilversteln

www.instagram.com/samsilverstein

www.facebook.com/silversteinsam

OTHER BOOKS BY SAM SILVERSTEIN

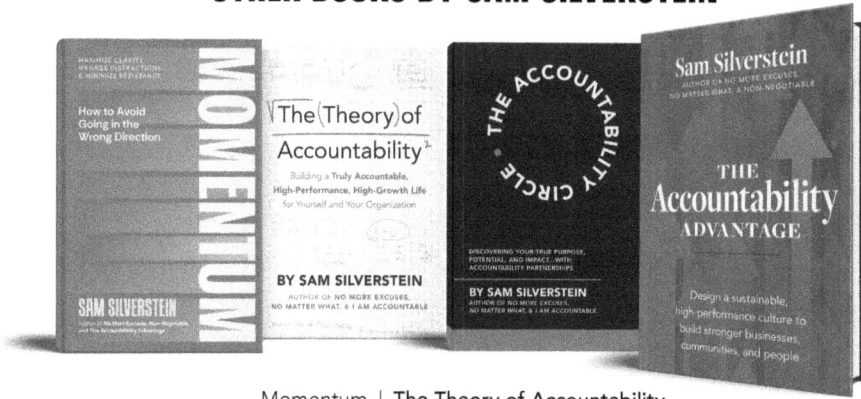

Momentum | The Theory of Accountability
The Accountability Circle | The Accountability Advantage

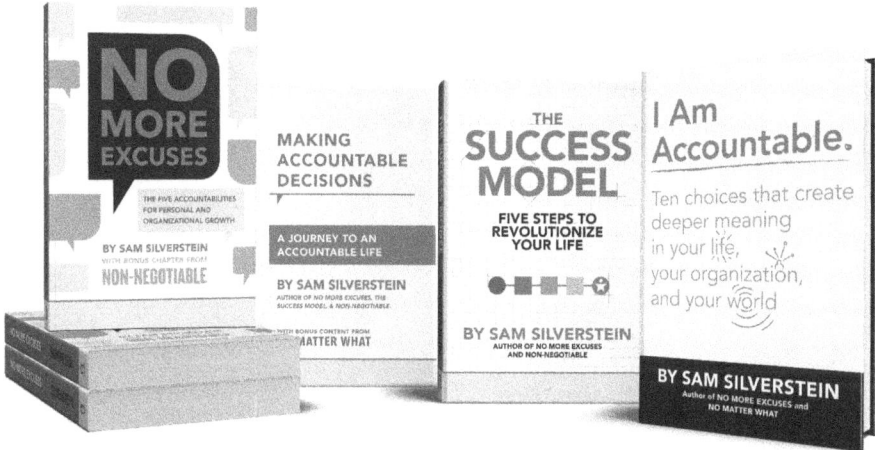

No More Excuses | Making Accountable Decisions | The Success Model | I Am Accountable

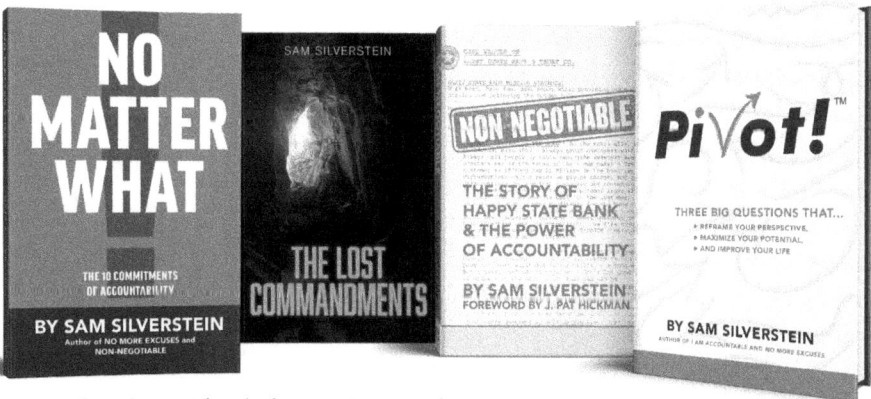

No Matter What | The Lost Commandments | Non Negotiable | Pivot!